Thinking about Content Reading

Dr. Kylene Beers

HOLT McDOUGAL

a division of Houghton Mifflin Harcourt

Kylene Beers, Ed.D.
Senior Reading Researcher
Comer School Development Program
Yale University
New Haven, Connecticut

Kylene Beers is a Senior Reading Researcher in the Comer School Development Program of the Child Study Center at Yale University. A former middle school teacher, Kylene has turned her commitment to helping struggling readers into the major focus of her research, writing, speaking, and teaching. She is a program author for *Holt Literature and Language Arts,* grades 6–12, and *Elements of Literature,* grades 6–12; author of *When Kids Can't Read/What Teachers Can Do* (Heinemann, 2002) and the forthcoming book *Thinking Through Reading: Comprehension, Fluency, and Vocabulary Strategies for Struggling Readers* (Heinemann, 2006); co-editor of *Into Focus: Understanding and Creating Middle School Readers* (Christopher-Gordon, 1998); and co-editor of *Books for You: An Annotated Booklist for High School Students* (NCTE, 2000). A respected authority on struggling readers who works with elementary, middle school, and high school teachers across the nation, Beers was the 2001 recipient of the Richard W. Halle Award given by NCTE for outstanding contributions to middle school education.

ISBN-13: 978-0-55-402393-9
ISBN-10: 0-55-402393-8

1 2 3 4 5 6 7 8 9 082 12 11 10 09 08

Contents

Thinking about Content Reading

To the Student

This book is designed to help you read your social studies books. It contains activities that will help you learn how to focus on important information and discover meaning as you read. This book has the following three parts:

- Reading Skills
- Think-Alouds
- Graphic Organizers

Each part focuses on specific skills or strategies you can use to improve your reading.

Reading Skills

This part begins with The Reading Process Chart that will guide you through all stages of the reading process. Here you will also find lessons that teach different reading skills, such as finding main ideas or comparing and contrasting. For each skill, read the page of explanation and follow along with the example. Then you can practice the skill on your own with the worksheets. These worksheets contain passages taken directly from your social studies book and graphic organizers to help you organize the information and your thinking as you read.

Think-Alouds

Think-Alouds are fun! When you do a Think-Aloud, you practice thinking about what you are reading. Thinking about your reading will help you make connections between the content and what you already know. Passages used in the Think-Alouds are taken directly from your social studies book. You can use the Think-Aloud examples in this book to see the kinds of comments other students have made as they have read. When you get the idea, you can use the Think-Aloud Comments Sheet to remind you to "think aloud" as you read any passage from your textbook.

Graphic Organizers

Graphic organizers are helpful for organizing information as you read. The How to Use Graphic Organizers chart at the end of this book shows several different types of graphic organizers, so you can choose the type that works best for whatever topic you are reading about. You can use these graphic organizers to take notes and as a study tool to help you prepare for important tests.

Thinking about Content Reading

Name _____ Class _____ Date _____

The Reading Process

Getting Ready to Read

Pilots go through a checklist before they begin flying. You too should use a checklist to make sure you are ready to read.

Titles
1. What's the title?
2. What predictions about content can I make from the title?
3. What predictions can I make from the subheadings?

Vocabulary
4. Is there a list of vocabulary words or key terms that I need to look over before I begin to read?
5. Did I divide the vocabulary words into words I know, words I've heard, words I don't know at all?

Special Features
6. What do the maps, charts, illustrations, or timelines tell me?
7. Did I review the information found in the section openers?
8. Can I state my purpose for reading this section? What am I supposed to be learning?

_____

Vocabulary to Learn

As I Read

Use the following questions to help clarify meaning as you read.

Visualizing: Can I picture this in my mind? What words help me create that picture?

Connecting: How is this (detail) like some other (detail)? How is this (person/character) like another?

Questioning: What part has confused me? What names or terms do I need to review? Can I put events in the right time order?

Clarifying: Should I reread? Read on? Can I point to where I'm confused? Can I explain what is confusing me? Should I look again at graphics? Would looking up a word in a dictionary help? Should I ask for some help?

Seeing Relationships: Do I understand the causes or effects of this event?

Predicting: Based on what I've read, what do I think will happen next? Are there signal words like *however, additionally, or in conclusion* that give me an idea of what's next?

Summarizing: Can I discuss what I've just read in my own words?

_____

I am confused about …

After I Read

Use this space to reflect on what you've read.

The main idea of this part was…

The summary of this section is…

Three questions I'd like to ask are
1.

2.

3.

A part where I'm still confused is…

Important dates or ideas from this section are…

Vocabulary, key terms, or names I need to review…

Thinking about Content Reading

When you go on a trip, you have a purpose or a destination in mind before you start. Sometimes you need a map to get to your destination. When you read, you should also have a purpose in mind. This purpose keeps you focused and moving toward your goal of understanding.

As you read your textbook, you may feel lost or like you are going to a completely new place. However, textbooks provide "maps," or clues, to help you figure out where you are going. These clues are text features, such as a chapter's title, headings, pictures, and study tips. Text features can help you set a purpose for your reading.

HOW TO SET A PURPOSE

To set a purpose, follow these three basic steps:

1. **Look over the text features in the section you are about to read.** Notice headings, outlines, margin notes, and pictures.

2. **Ask yourself questions based on the text features.** Find something that interests you and then ask yourself a question about the topic.

3. **Set a purpose to guide your reading and answer your questions.** Your purpose might start out like this: "I'll read to find out about . . ."

President Adams and the XYZ Affair

When the diplomats arrived in France, they learned that French foreign minister Talleyrand would not speak with them. Instead, they had a strange and secret visit from three French agents. Shockingly, the agents said that Talleyrand would discuss a treaty only in exchange for a $250,000 bribe. The French government also wanted a loan of $12 million. The amazed diplomats refused these demands.

In March 1798 President Adams told Congress that the peace-seeking mission had failed. He described the French terms, substituting the letters X, Y, and Z for the names of the French agents. Upon hearing the disgraceful news, Federalists in Congress called for war with France.

The XYZ affair, as the French demand for a bribe came to be called, outraged the American public.

1. Notice text features such as headings, pictures, or tips.
This heading mentions President Adams and some affair involving letters.

2. Ask questions about the text features.
I wonder what the XYZ affair is. How did it get such a strange name? What was its impact?

3. Set a purpose for your reading.
I'll read to find out more about the XYZ affair.

From *United States History*, Launching the Nation

Setting a Purpose

Reading Skills

Reading United States History

As you read about United States history you will come across a lot of new information. Setting a purpose can help keep you focused and moving toward your goal of understanding.

YOU TRY IT!

Use text features to help you set a purpose that will guide your reading. Complete the graphic organizer to help you through the steps of setting a purpose.

Devastation in the Dust Bowl

In the midst of the economic disaster, nature delivered a cruel blow. Around 1931 much of the Great Plains region entered a long, severe dry spell. This drought, or period of below-average rainfall, lasted for several years. By the time it lifted, millions of people had fled the area.

The great dust storms Drought is a part of a weather cycle, naturally occurring on the Great Plains every few decades. By the 1930s, however, careless agricultural practices had left the region vulnerable. Land once covered with grasses now lay bare to the sky with no vegetation to hold the soil in place.

When the storms came, they stripped away the topsoil and blew it hundreds of miles away. In some of the worst storms, dust reached as far as the Atlantic Coast. Drifting mounds of dust choked crops and buried farm equipment. The fine dust blew into homes through drafty windows and under doors. Year after year, storms came and wreaked destruction. The hardest hit area—including parts of Oklahoma, Kansas, Colorado, New Mexico, and Texas—became known as the Dust Bowl.

From *American Anthem*, The Great Depression Begins

Pick a heading that interests you.

_____
_____
_____
_____
_____
_____

▼

Ask yourself a question about the heading.

_____
_____
_____
_____
_____
_____

▼

Set a purpose for your reading.

_____
_____
_____
_____
_____
_____
_____

Thinking about Content Reading

Setting a Purpose

As you read about world history you will come across a lot of new information. Setting a purpose can help keep you focused and moving toward your goal of understanding.

YOU TRY IT!

Use text features to help you set a purpose that will guide your reading. Complete the graphic organizer to help you through the steps of setting a purpose.

Section 3: Greek Mythology and Literature

What You Will Learn . . .
Main Ideas

1. The Greeks created myths to explain the world.
2. Ancient Greek literature provides some of the world's greatest poems and stories.
3. Greek literature lives in and influences our world even today.

The Big Idea

The ancient Greeks created great myths and works of literature that influence the way we speak and write today.

Key Terms and People

mythology
Homer
Sappho
Aesop
fables

Building Background

The Greeks lived in a time long before the development of science. To them, natural events like thunderstorms and changing seasons were mysterious. Today we can explain what causes these events. But to the Greeks, they seemed like the work of powerful gods.

From *World History*, Ancient Greece

Pick a text feature that interests you.

_____
_____
_____
_____
_____
_____
_____

▼

Ask yourself a question about the text feature.

_____
_____
_____
_____
_____
_____
_____

▼

Set a purpose for your reading.

_____
_____
_____
_____
_____
_____
_____

Setting a Purpose

Reading Skills
Reading Geography

As you read about geography you will come across a lot of new information. Setting a purpose can help keep you focused and moving toward your goal of understanding.

YOU TRY IT!

Use text features to help you set a purpose that will guide your reading. Complete the graphic organizer to help you through the steps of setting a purpose.

Section 3: East Africa Today

What You Will Learn . . .
Main Ideas

1. National parks are a major source of income for Tanzania and Kenya.
2. Rwanda and Burundi are densely populated rural countries with a history of ethnic conflict.
3. Both Sudan and Uganda have economies based on agriculture, but Sudan has suffered from years of war.
4. The countries of the Horn of Africa are among the poorest in the world.

The Big Idea

East Africa has abundant national parks, but most of the region's countries are poor and recovering from conflicts.

Building Background

Many of the countries of East Africa are rich in natural resources—including wildlife—but people disagree about the best way to use them. Droughts can make life here difficult. In addition, political and ethnic conflicts have led to unrest and violence in some areas of the region.

From *Africa*, East Africa

Pick a text feature that interests you.

_____
_____
_____
_____
_____

Ask yourself a question about the text feature.

_____
_____
_____
_____
_____
_____

Set a purpose for your reading.

_____
_____
_____
_____
_____
_____

Thinking about Content Reading

Setting a Purpose

As you read about civics and government you will come across a lot of new information. Setting a purpose can help keep you focused and moving toward your goal of understanding.

YOU TRY IT!

Use text features to help you set a purpose that will guide your reading. Complete the graphic organizer to help you through the steps of setting a purpose.

The President's Roles

The Constitution states that "the executive power shall be vested in [given to] a President of the United States of America. This power applies to several areas of the government, including the military and foreign policy.

Legislative Leader The president recommends, or suggests, new laws to Congress. Every year the president delivers a State of the Union Address to Congress. Usually presented in late January, this televised speech sets forth the programs and policies that the president wants Congress to put into effect as laws. These programs and policies usually address the country's most pressing concerns. The president also sends Congress a budget proposing how the federal government should raise and spend money. In this budget, the president recommends laws and programs to help the economy. The legislature often does not follow the president's budget plan.

The president also influences Congress by indicating what legislation he or she does not want. One powerful way for the president to do this is by using the veto. This tactic is so effective that just the threat of a presidential veto often discourages Congress from passing a bill. It takes a two-thirds vote of both houses of Congress to override a veto, or pass a bill after a president has vetoed it.

From *Civics in Practice*, The Executive Branch

Pick a text feature that interests you.

_____
_____
_____
_____
_____
_____
_____

▼

Ask yourself a question about the text feature.

_____
_____
_____
_____
_____
_____
_____

▼

Set a purpose for your reading.

_____
_____
_____
_____
_____
_____
_____

Setting a Purpose

Reading Skills
Reading Economics

As you read about economics you will come across a lot of new information. Setting a purpose can help keep you focused and moving toward your goal of understanding.

YOU TRY IT!

Use text features to help you set a purpose that will guide your reading. Complete the graphic organizer to help you through the steps of setting a purpose.

Economic Decisions

How does an economist view the world? Economists pay attention to economic decisions, observing not only who makes them but also how those decisions are made.

Who Makes Decisions? You do! You may choose to buy concert tickets or to start a tutoring business. The people around you also make decisions, as do people around the world.

In economic terms, there are two large groups of economic decision makers. The people who decide to buy things are called consumers. The people who make the things that satisfy consumers' needs and wants are called producers. Consumers choose what to buy, and producers choose what to provide and how to provide it. This network of decisions is the basis of all economic systems. Every society around the world has an economic system whether that society consists of a neighborhood or a nation.

From *Holt Economics*, What Is Economics?

Pick a text feature that interests you.

_____
_____
_____
_____
_____
_____
_____

Ask yourself a question about the text feature.

_____
_____
_____
_____
_____
_____

Set a purpose for your reading.

_____
_____
_____
_____
_____
_____
_____

Thinking about Content Reading

Have you ever been caught up in a mystery novel or TV show? As you follow the clues, sometimes you can solve the crime before the book or the show ends. When you do that, you are making a prediction, or a guess about what will happen next.

Making predictions can also help you as you read social studies. Predicting helps you to stay involved with your reading as you try to find out whether your prediction was right.

HOW TO MAKE PREDICTIONS

To make predictions, follow these four basic steps:

1. **Rely on information that you already know.** As you read social studies, think of what you already know about people, places, events, and other subjects.

2. **Add new information from your reading.** Your textbook will provide new information that you should consider along with what you already know.

3. **Form a prediction that makes sense.** Put the old and new information together to make a prediction. In social studies, your predictions will focus on what you think might have happened next or what life was like in different cultures or at different times.

4. **Confirm or adjust your prediction.** As you continue reading, you will see how accurate your prediction was. If necessary, you can adjust it and move on to the next prediction.

Physical Features

Eastern Europe is a land of amazing contrasts. The northern parts of the region lie along the cold, often stormy shores of the Baltic Sea. In the south, however, are warm, sunny beaches along the Adriatic and Black seas. Jagged mountain peaks jut high into the sky in some places, while wildflowers dot the gently rolling hills of other parts of the region. These contrasts stem from the region's wide variety of landforms, water features, and climates.

From *Europe and Russia*, Eastern Europe

1. Take what you already know.	2. Add new information from your reading.	3. Form predictions that make sense.	4. Confirm or adjust your prediction.
I know places with warm, sunny beaches are popular with tourists.	There are warm beaches along the Adriatic and Black seas.	The warm beaches of Eastern Europe probably attract many tourists.	Ah ha! A few pages later the textbook says that the region's beaches are popular with tourists.

Making Predictions

Reading Skills

Reading United States History

As you read about United States history you will come across a lot of new information. Making predictions can help you stay involved with your reading as you see whether your prediction was right.

YOU TRY IT!

Read the following passage about the counterculture of the 1960s. As you read, think about what you already know about teens, rebellion, and hippies. Then predict in what ways the teens and young adults expressed their rebellion.

Rise of the Counterculture

The counterculture of the 1960s was a rebellion of teens and young adults against mainstream American society. These young Americans, called hippies, believed that society's values were hollow and its priorities were misplaced. Turning their backs on the mainstream—which they called the establishment—hippies wanted to create an alternative culture based on peace and love.

Where did the counterculture come from? First of all, the number of teens and young adults in the United States rose dramatically in the 1960s. Between 1960 and 1970 the number of Americans aged 15 through 24 increased almost 50 percent.

From *American Anthem*, A Time of Social Change

What I already know	**New information I read**	**My prediction**
_____	_____	_____
_____	_____	_____
_____	_____	_____
_____	_____	_____
_____	_____	_____
_____	_____	_____
_____	_____	_____

Making Predictions

As you read about world history you will come across a lot of new information. Making predictions can help you stay involved with your reading as you see whether your prediction was right.

YOU TRY IT!

Read the following passage about how the church influenced art during the Middle Ages. As you read, think about what you already know about art and religion. Then predict what kind of objects artists might have created during the Middle Ages.

The Church and the Arts

In addition to politics and education, the church was also a strong influence on art and architecture. Throughout the Middle Ages, religious feeling inspired artists and architects to create beautiful works of art.

Religious Architecture Many of Europe's churches were incredible works of art. The grandest of these churches were cathedrals, large churches in which bishops led religious services. Beginning in the 1100s Europeans built their cathedrals using a dramatic new style called Gothic architecture.

Gothic cathedrals were not only places to pray, but also symbols of people's faith. As a result, they were towering works of great majesty and glory.

From *World History*, The Later Middle Ages

What I already know	New information I read	My prediction

Making Predictions

Reading Skills
Reading Geography

As you read about geography you will come across a lot of new information. Making predictions can help you stay involved with your reading as you see whether your prediction was right.

YOU TRY IT!

Read the following passage about population growth in Kenya. As you read, think about what you already know about population growth. Then predict what kinds of challenges Kenya might face because of its population explosion.

Population Growth in Kenya

If the current growth rate continues, the world's population will grow by almost a billion people every 12 years! Countries where big families bring high status and ensure care for elders later in life have the highest growth rates. In addition, farming families often want many children so they can work in the fields. All these factors apply to Kenya. In 1988 Kenya had a population growth rate of 4.2 percent— the highest any country has ever recorded. Kenya's growth rate soared because more children were born, fewer children died, and modern medicine kept more people alive longer.

After Kenya won independence in 1963, the country's economy expanded quickly. However, by the 1980s the economy could no longer keep pace with the population. Too many resources went just to supply the needs of the huge population. Little was left over for development.

From *World Geography Today*, East Africa

What I already know	New information I read	My prediction
_____	_____	_____
_____	_____	_____
_____	_____	_____
_____	_____	_____
_____	_____	_____
_____	_____	_____
_____	_____	_____

Making Predictions

Reading Skills
Reading Civics

As you read about civics and government you will come across a lot of new information. Making predictions can help you stay involved with your reading as you see whether your prediction was right.

YOU TRY IT!

Read the following passage about Congress. As you read, think about what you already know about laws that affect your life. Then predict what kinds of laws Congress has the authority to make.

The Powers of Congress

The U.S. Congress is the most powerful representative body in the world. Under the Constitution, Congress's most important responsibility is to make laws. These laws do not simply tell us what we can and cannot do. They affect us in other ways as well. For example, laws passed by Congress determine how high taxes will be. They provide for the building of highways and dams. They determine what military equipment the United States will sell to other countries. The actions of Congress affect the lives of millions of people in the United States and throughout the world.

From *Civics in Practice*, The Legislative Branch

What I already know	New information I read	My prediction

Making Predictions

Reading Skills

Reading Economics

As you read about economics you will come across a lot of new information. Making predictions can help you stay involved with your reading as you see whether your prediction was right.

YOU TRY IT!

Read the following passage about the law of demand. As you read, think about what you already know about demand. Then predict how increases and decreases in price might affect demand.

Law of Demand

In a free-enterprise system, price is the main variable affecting demand. Specifically there is an inverse or opposite, relationship between price and the quantity demanded. This relationship is described by the law of demand, which states that an increase in a good's price causes a decrease in the quantity demanded and that a decrease in price causes an increase in the quantity demanded.

Suppose that you want to buy a compact disc (CD) player. You expect to buy a CD player for about $200, and you have saved that amount. One Saturday you go to the Avalon Electronics store. When you arrive at the store, you discover that the price of CD players has increased from $200 to $300. You are not able to pay $300 for a CD player because you have not saved that much money. Even if you were able to pay the higher price, you might not be willing to do so. Similarly, some other consumers also will be unwilling or unable to buy CD players at the higher price.

From *Holt Economics*, Demand

What I already know		New information I read		My prediction
_____	▶	_____	▶	_____
_____		_____		_____
_____		_____		_____
_____		_____		_____
_____		_____		_____
_____		_____		_____

A main idea is like the hub of a wheel. The hub holds the wheel together, and everything circles around it. In a paragraph, the main idea holds the information together. All the facts and details revolve around the main idea.

Why do we bother to look for main ideas? Social studies is not just a bunch of facts. Instead, it is about facts and their meanings. When we find main ideas, we find the meaning behind the details.

HOW TO IDENTIFY MAIN IDEAS AND DETAILS

To identify a main idea and details, follow these three basic steps:

1. **Identify the topic of the paragraph.** Ask yourself, "What is this paragraph mostly about?"

2. **Note important facts and details that relate to the topic.** The details help you understand something about the topic of the paragraph.

3. **Determine the main idea.** The main idea is the main point about the topic. It shapes the paragraph's content and the meaning of all the facts and details in it. Sometimes the main idea is stated clearly in a sentence. Other times the main idea is only suggested, not stated.

City Growth

A number of different factors have influenced the site and growth of cities. One is location near key resources. Other factors include location along transportation and trade routes and at easily defended sites. Many of the world's greatest cities grew up where two or three of these factors were present. Once cities are established, continued access to other cities and resources allows them to grow and prosper.

From *World Geography Today*, Human Systems

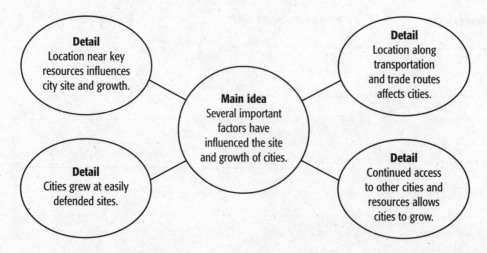

Detail
Location near key resources influences city site and growth.

Detail
Location along transportation and trade routes affects cities.

Main idea
Several important factors have influenced the site and growth of cities.

Detail
Cities grew at easily defended sites.

Detail
Continued access to other cities and resources allows cities to grow.

Identifying Main Ideas and Details

Reading Skills

Reading United States History

As you read about United States history you will come across a lot of new information. To make sure you grasp important points as you read, practice identifying the main idea and details. That way you will know you are focusing on the right information.

YOU TRY IT!

Read the following passage. Then fill in the chart on the next page with the main idea and supporting details. Remember, the main idea might not always be stated in the paragraph.

Industry Changes Society

Every time motorists turned the crank handle to start their cars, other industries benefited. Demand for steel, glass, rubber, and other automobile materials soared. Automobile repair shops and filling stations sprang up in cities and towns. Motels and restaurants arose to meet the needs of car travelers.

From *American Anthem*, From War to Peace

Main Idea and Details Chart

MAIN IDEA

↓

SUPPORTING DETAIL 1
SUPPORTING DETAIL 2
SUPPORTING DETAIL 3

Identifying Main Ideas and Details

As you read about world history you will come across a lot of new information. To make sure you grasp important points as you read, practice identifying the main idea and details. That way you will know you are focusing on the right information.

YOU TRY IT!

Read the following passage. Then fill in the chart on the next page with the main idea and supporting details. Remember, the main idea might not always be stated in the paragraph.

Disorder in the Republic

Rome in the 70s BC was a dangerous place. Politicians and generals went to war to increase their power even as political order broke down in Rome. There were politically inspired riots to restore the power of the tribunes. All the while, more and more people from throughout the republic flooded into the city, further adding to the confusion.

From *World History*, Rome and Christianity

Main Idea and Details Chart

MAIN IDEA

SUPPORTING DETAIL 1
SUPPORTING DETAIL 2
SUPPORTING DETAIL 3

Identifying Main Ideas and Details

Reading Skills

Reading Geography

As you read about geography you will come across a lot of new information. To make sure you grasp important points as you read, practice identifying the main idea and details. That way you will know you are focusing on the right information.

YOU TRY IT!

Read the following passage. Then fill in the chart on the next page with the main idea and supporting details. Remember, the main idea might not always be stated in the paragraph.

Culture

Because of their shared history, Ireland and Great Britain share many cultural features. Social life is often centered around local eateries. Sports such as soccer, rugby, and cricket are popular. In addition, English is the main language of both countries. However a small number of Irish also speak Irish Gaelic, and some Scots speak Scottish Gaelic.

From *World Geography Today*, Northern and Western Europe

Main Idea and Details Chart

MAIN IDEA

$\downarrow$

SUPPORTING DETAIL 1
SUPPORTING DETAIL 2
SUPPORTING DETAIL 3

Identifying Main Ideas and Details

As you read about civics and government you will come across a lot of new information. To make sure you grasp important points as you read, practice identifying the main idea and details. That way you will know you are focusing on the right information.

YOU TRY IT!

Read the following passage. Then fill in the chart on the next page with the main idea and supporting details. Remember, the main idea might not always be stated in the paragraph.

Organization of the House of Representatives

The person who presides over the House when it is in session is called the Speaker of the House. The Speaker, who is always a member of the majority party, is the most powerful officer in the House. For example, no representative may speak until called on, or recognized, by the Speaker. The Speaker also influences the order of business in the House.

From *Civics in Practice*, The Legislative Branch

Main Idea and Details Chart

MAIN IDEA

↓

SUPPORTING DETAIL 1

SUPPORTING DETAIL 2

SUPPORTING DETAIL 3

Identifying Main Ideas and Details

Reading Skills

Reading Economics

As you read about economics you will come across a lot of new information. To make sure you grasp important points as you read, practice identifying the main idea and details. That way you will know you are focusing on the right information.

YOU TRY IT!

Read the following passage. Then fill in the chart on the next page with the main idea and supporting details. Remember, the main idea might not always be stated in the paragraph.

Scarcity

All resources are limited. People's wants however, are unlimited. This combination of limited economic resources and unlimited wants results in a condition known as scarcity. Scarcity is the most basic problem of economics, because it forces people to make decisions about how to use resources effectively.

Many factors contribute to scarcity. Low amounts of rainfall, for example, may lead to poor harvests and therefore to scarcity of fruits and vegetables at grocery stores. During World War II, silk and nylon were used to make parachutes—creating a scarcity of women's stockings, which had been produced from those materials during peacetime.

From *Holt Economics*, What Is Economics?

Main Idea and Details Chart

MAIN IDEA

↓

SUPPORTING DETAIL 1

SUPPORTING DETAIL 2

SUPPORTING DETAIL 3

Maybe you have watched a TV commercial and enjoyed the fast-moving pictures, music, and dialogue. Suppose that as you flip through a magazine, you come across the same ad. You see that the TV commercial has been stripped down to the most important details. The magazine ad is a summary of the TV commercial.

As you read social studies, you can use a summary to help you focus on and remember what you read. A summary is like the magazine ad. It is a short restatement, or stripped-down version, of the most important points of the text.

To create a summary, follow three basic steps.

1. **Underline the important details in the passage.** Look for ideas, names, places, and other facts that get right to the meat of the passage.

2. **Write one or two sentences that summarize the important details in the paragraph or passage.** As you summarize, you may realize that you need to delete or add information. Try to make your summary both short and complete.

3. **Combine these paragraph summaries into a short summary of the whole passage.** Try to be as concise as possible, but don't leave out important information. Your summary should jog your memory of the entire passage.

Historians and archaeologists have known about <u>hieroglyphics for centuries</u>, but for a long time <u>they didn't know how to read it</u>. In fact, it was not until <u>1799</u> when <u>a lucky discovery</u> by a French soldier <u>gave historians the key</u> they needed to read ancient Egyptian writing.

That key was the <u>Rosetta Stone, a huge, stone slab inscribed with hieroglyphics</u>. In addition to the hieroglyphics, <u>the Rosetta Stone had text in Greek</u> and a later form of Egyptian. Because the text in all three languages was the same, <u>scholars who knew Greek were able to figure out what the hieroglyphics said</u>.

From *World History*, Ancient Egypt and Kush

Summary of Paragraph 1
A lucky discovery in 1799 helped historians read hieroglyphics for the first time in centuries.

▼

Summary of Paragraph 2
The Rosetta Stone had the same text written in both Greek and hieroglyphics that Greek scholars could read.

▼

Combined Summary
Scholars were finally able to read hieroglyphics in 1799 when the Rosetta Stone was discovered. It had a passage written in both Greek and hierogpyphics.

Summarizing

As you read about United States history, you will come across a lot of new information. Summarizing can help you focus on and remember what you read.

YOU TRY IT!

Read the following passage and underline the important points. Then fill out the graphic organizer below to create a summary. The first box has been completed for you.

The Nuremberg Trials

Following World War II, many of the Nazis believed to be responsible for the Final Solution and the concentration camps were put on trial. The court was called the International Military Tribunal. It was organized by the United States, Great Britain, France, and the Soviet Union.

A total of 22 Nazis were tried for war crimes. Included were some of the leading figures of the Nazi movement, including Hermann Goering. Twelve were sentenced to die. Several others served long prison terms.

In addition, following this trial, several other Nazis were captured and tried in different courts. These trials demonstrated the commitment of people around the world to remember the terrible experience of the Jews at the hands of the Nazis—known today as the Holocaust.

From *American Anthem*, The United States in World War II

Summary of Paragraph 1
A trial called the International Military Tribunal was held after World War II to try Nazis for war crimes.

▼

Summary of Paragraph 2
_____
_____
_____
_____

▼

Summary of Paragraph 3
_____
_____
_____
_____

▼

Combined Summary
_____
_____
_____
_____
_____
_____

Thinking about Content Reading

Summarizing

Reading Skills

Reading World History

As you read about world history you will come across a lot of new information. Summarizing can help you focus on and remember what you read.

YOU TRY IT!

Read the following passage and underline the important points. Then fill out the graphic organizer below to create a summary. The first box has been completed for you.

Scrolls Reveal Past Beliefs

Besides the Torah, the Hebrew Bible, and the Commentaries, many other documents explain ancient Jewish beliefs. Among the most important are the Dead Sea Scrolls, writings by Jews who lived about 2,000 years ago.

Until 1947 no one knew about the Dead Sea Scrolls. In that year, young boys looking for a lost goat near the Dead Sea found a small cave. One of the boys went in to explore and found several old jars filled with moldy scrolls.

Scholars were very excited about the boys' find. Eager to find more scrolls, they began to search the desert. Over the next few decades, searchers found several more groups of scrolls.

Careful study revealed that most of the Dead Sea Scrolls were written between 100 BC and AD 50. The scrolls included prayers, commentaries, letters, and passages from the Hebrew Bible. These writings help historians learn about the lives of many Jews during this time.

From *World History*, The Hebrews and Judaism

Summary of Paragraph 1
The Dead Sea scrolls, which were written 2,000 years ago, help explain ancient Jewish beliefs.

▼

Summary of Paragraph 2
_____
_____
_____

▼

Summary of Paragraph 3
_____
_____
_____

▼

Summary of Paragraph 4
_____
_____
_____

▼

Combined Summary
_____
_____
_____
_____
_____

Summarizing

As you read about geography you will come across a lot of new information. Summarizing can help you focus on and remember what you read.

YOU TRY IT!

Read the following passage and underline the important points. Then fill out the graphic organizer below to create a summary. The first box has been completed for you.

The Moscow Region

Moscow, with its huge Kremlin, has symbolized Russia for centuries. The city became the home of the Russian Orthodox Church in the 1300s and Russia's capital in the 1400s. Most Russians have looked to Moscow as their country's heart and soul. This was true even while St. Petersburg was the capital from 1712 to 1918.

Today Greater Moscow is Russia's most important economic region. It is the national center of communications, culture, education, finance, politics, and transportation. More than 70 institutions of higher learning are there. As a result, Moscow's economic advantages are many. Roads, rails, and air routes link the capital to all points in Russia. The city's location also gives its businesses access to raw materials and labor.

The economic region around Moscow stretches for many miles in all directions. Millions of Russians live and work within the area's network of transportation routes and job sites. Among the transportation links is the world's busiest subway. The area also has electrified railroads and a major beltway.

From *World Geography Today*, Russia, Ukraine, and Belorus

Summary of Paragraph 1
Russians love Moscow, the country's capital and religious center.

▼

Summary of Paragraph 2
_____
_____
_____
_____

▼

Summary of Paragraph 3
_____
_____
_____
_____

▼

Combined Summary
_____
_____
_____
_____
_____
_____
_____

Summarizing

As you read about civics and government you will come across a lot of new information. Summarizing can help you focus on and remember what you read.

YOU TRY IT!
Read the following passage and underline the important points. Then fill out the graphic organizer below to create a summary. The first box has been completed for you.

Propaganda and Public Opinion

Many of the ideas in the mass media have been directed at us for a purpose. Someone or some group is urging us to do something—to buy something, to believe something, or to act in a certain way. Ideas that are spread to influence people are called propaganda.

It has been said that we live in the propaganda age. Propaganda is certainly nothing new, but it has become increasingly influential in recent years. Two reasons for this development are the tremendous growth of the mass media and advances in communications technology. Communications satellites, computer networks, and television broadcasts all help spread propaganda farther and faster than ever before.

There are always many people, groups, and advertisers using propaganda to influence public opinion. Advertisers use propaganda to urge consumers to buy their products. Political candidates use propaganda to convince voters to support them.

From *Civics in Practice*, The Political System

Summary of Paragraph 1
The mass media often uses propaganda to influence people to act or believe in a certain way.

▼

Summary of Paragraph 2
_____
_____
_____

▼

Summary of Paragraph 3
_____
_____
_____

▼

Combined Summary
_____
_____
_____
_____
_____

Summarizing

As you read about economics you will come across a lot of new information. Summarizing can help you focus on and remember what you read.

YOU TRY IT!

Read the following passage and underline the important points. Then fill out the graphic organizer below to create a summary. The first box has been completed for you.

An Economic Way of Thinking

How do you decide what food to eat, what clothes to wear, and what movies to see? The study of the choices that people make to meet their needs and wants is called economics. A person who studies these economic choices is called an economist.

Economists generally classify economic actions into categories: microeconomics and macroeconomics. Microeconomics is the study of the choices made by economic actors such as households, companies, and individual markets. Although the term micro means "small," microeconomics can focus on large participants in the economy. For example, the production at one company—even one as large as Exxon Mobil Corporation, whose total output exceeds that of some nations—is considered a microeconomic topic because only a single economic actor is involved.

Macroeconomics on the other hand, examines the behavior of entire economies. For example, unemployment in the United States is a macroeconomic topic.

From *Holt Economics*, What Is Economics?

Summary of Paragraph 1
Economists study economics, the study of the choices people make to meet their needs and wants.

▼

Summary of Paragraph 2
_____
_____
_____
_____

▼

Summary of Paragraph 3
_____
_____
_____
_____

▼

Combined Summary
_____
_____
_____
_____
_____
_____

What is the difference between a good guess and a weak guess?
A good guess is an educated guess. In other words, the guess is based
on some knowledge or information. An educated guess is sometimes
called an inference.

Sometimes reading well means understanding what the writer does not
tell you as well as what the writer does tell you. Making inferences can
help you understand and make connections with the text.

HOW TO MAKE INFERENCES
To make inferences, follow these four basic steps:

1. **Ask a question that the text does not directly answer.** Pick a topic that interests
   you. What does the writer not tell you about this topic?

2. **Note information "inside the text."** If you chose a good question, your textbook
   will provide clues to the question.

3. **Note information "outside the text."** Think about what you already know about
   the subject from earlier reading or from your own experience.

4. **Use both sets of information to make an educated guess, or inference.**
   Combine what you read with what you already know. With this full set of information, you should be able to figure out what the writer does not tell you.

Northern Draft

In March 1863, war critics erupted again when
Congress approved a draft, or forced military service. For $300, men were allowed to buy their way
out of military service. For an unskilled laborer,
however, that was nearly a year's wages. Critics of
the draft called the Civil War a "rich man's war and
a poor man's fight."

From *United States History*, The Civil War

1. Question
Why were people critical of the draft?

▼

2. Information "inside the text"
- Men could buy their way out of military service.
- The fee to get out of military service was very high for unskilled laborers.
- Critics called it a rich man's war and a poor man's fight.

▼

3. Information "outside the text"
- A draft means they were probably having a hard time getting people to fight.
- $300 was a lot of money back then.

▼

4. Inference
Critics thought the draft was unfair to poor people.

Making Inferences

Reading Skills
Reading United States History

As you read about United States history you will come across a lot of new information. Making inferences shows that you can apply your knowledge as you read.

YOU TRY IT!

Read the following passage. Combine information you read with what you already know to make an inference about the earliest battles of the Civil War.

Training the Soldiers

Both the Union and Confederate armies faced shortages of clothing, food, and even rifles. Most troops lacked standard uniforms and simply wore their own clothes. Eventually, each side chose a color for their uniforms. The Union chose blue. The Confederates wore gray.

The problem with volunteers was that many of them had no idea how to fight. Schoolteachers, farmers, and laborers all had to learn the combat basics of marching, shooting, and using bayonets.

With visions of glory and action, many young soldiers were eager to fight. They would not have to wait long.

Discipline and drill were used to turn raw volunteers into an efficient fighting machine. During a battle, the success or failure of a regiment often depended on its discipline—how well it responded to orders.

Volunteers also learned how to use rifles. Eventually, soldiers were expected to be able to load, aim, and fire their rifles three times in one minute. The quality of the weapons provided varied greatly.

From *United States History*, The Civil War

Question
What were the earliest battles of the Civil War probably like?

▼

Information "inside the text"
_____
_____
_____
_____
_____
_____
_____

▼

Information "outside the text"
_____
_____
_____
_____
_____
_____
_____

▼

Inference
_____
_____
_____
_____

Making Inferences

Reading Skills

Reading World History

As you read about world history you will come across a lot of new information. Making inferences shows that you can apply your knowledge as you read.

YOU TRY IT!

Read the following passage. Combine information you read with what you already know to make an inference about why the Aryans did not build big cities.

Government and Society

As nomads, the Aryans took along their herds of animals as they moved. But over time, they settled in villages and began to farm. Unlike the Harappans, they did not build big cities.

The Aryan political system was also different from the Harappan system. The Aryans lived in small communities, based mostly on family ties. No single ruling authority existed. Instead, each group had its own leader, often a skilled warrior.

Aryan villages were governed by rajas. A raja was a leader who ruled a village and the land around it. Villagers farmed some of this land for the raja. They used other sections as pastures for their cows, horses, sheep, and goats.

Although many rajas were related, they didn't always get along. Sometimes rajas joined forces before fighting a common enemy. Other times, however, rajas went to war against each other. In fact, Aryan groups fought each other nearly as often as they fought outsiders.

From *World History*, Ancient India

Question
Why did the Aryans not build big cities like the Harappans did?

▼

Information "inside the text"
_____
_____
_____
_____
_____
_____

▼

Information "outside the text"
_____
_____
_____
_____
_____
_____

▼

Inference
_____
_____
_____
_____

Making Inferences

Reading Skills

Reading Geography

As you read about geography you will come across a lot of new information. Making inferences shows that you can apply your knowledge as you read.

YOU TRY IT!

Read the following passage. Combine information you read with what you already know to make an inference about when tourists are most likely to visit Central America and the Caribbean islands.

Climates, Plants, and Animals

Central America and the Caribbean islands extend across the sunny and warm tropical latitudes. Tropical wet and dry climates are typical. Temperatures seldom vary more than 10°F between summer and winter. During winter, high pressure generally brings dry weather. A summer rainy season results when low pressure cells begin to move north across the region. Rain can then be expected almost every afternoon. However, the region's physical features cause this general climate pattern to vary.

From *World Geography Today*, Central America and the Caribbean

---

Question
What is the busiest season for tourism in Central America and the Caribbean?

▼

Information "inside the text"
_____
_____
_____
_____
_____
_____
_____

▼

Information "outside the text"
_____
_____
_____
_____
_____
_____
_____

▼

Inference
_____
_____
_____
_____
_____

Thinking about Content Reading

Making Inferences

As you read about civics and government you will come across a lot of new information. Making inferences shows that you can apply your knowledge as you read.

YOU TRY IT!

Read the following passage. Combine information you read with what you already know to make an inference about why governments in some countries might not allow freedom of speech.

Freedom of Speech

"Congress shall make no law . . . abridging (limiting) the freedom of speech." This passage protects the right to express our ideas and opinions openly, as well as to listen to the speech of others. It means that we may talk freely to friends and neighbors or deliver a public speech. Free speech seems perfectly natural to us, but in some countries, free speech is severely limited.

One reason free speech is so important is that it allows us the freedom to criticize our government and government officials. People who live under a totalitarian government can be punished for criticizing their leaders.

There are limits to free-speech rights, however. You may not use your free speech rights in a way that could cause physical harm to others. For example, you do not have the right to yell "Fire!" in a crowded room just for fun. Yelling "Fire!" could cause a panic and get people hurt.

From *Civics in Practice*, Rights and Responsibilities

Question
Why do governments in some countries punish people for criticizing their leaders?

▼

Information "inside the text"
_____
_____
_____
_____
_____
_____

▼

Information "outside the text"
_____
_____
_____
_____
_____
_____

▼

Inference
_____
_____
_____
_____

Thinking about Content Reading

Making Inferences   Reading Skills

Reading Economics

As you read about economics you will come across a lot of new information. Making inferences shows that you can apply your knowledge as you read.

YOU TRY IT!
Read the following passage. Combine information you read with what you already know to make an inference about why people should avoid credit abuse.

Credit Abuse

Increasingly, credit abuse has become a problem for both consumers and businesses. Consumers sometimes take on more credit debt than they can handle. When repayment of loans and credit debts becomes a problem, consumers usually have two courses of action. First, they can seek credit counseling. Counselors advise consumers on ways to pay off present debts through a repayment program and how to avoid recurring credit problems.

Counselors sometimes advise people with severe credit problems to take out a debt consolidation loan to repay several smaller loans and credit balances. Debt consolidation loans carry high interest rates because of the high risk they pose to creditors.

Second, consumers with large debts may be advised to declare bankruptcy. Bankruptcy is a legal declaration of inability to pay debts. Those who have abused credit, particularly individuals, usually declare bankruptcy only as a last resort, for it has serious consequences. By law, bankruptcy information remains on a person's credit history for 14 years, making it nearly impossible for the person to borrow money or receive credit.

From *Holt Economics*, Sources of Capital

Question
Why should people avoid credit abuse?

▼

Information "inside the text"
_____
_____
_____
_____
_____
_____

▼

Information "outside the text"
_____
_____
_____
_____
_____
_____

▼

Inference
_____
_____
_____
_____

Most stories have a beginning, a middle, and an end. The information you read in your social studies books is no different. Identifying the correct sequence, or order, of events is important to understanding what you read.

As you read your textbook, you may find that you need to identify a sequence of events in order to understand what really took place. Developing a sequence chain is a good way to help you identify and understand the order of events.

HOW TO IDENTIFY SEQUENCE

To put events in sequence, follow these three basic steps:

1. **Look for dates or clue words that signal sequence.** Words such as *first*, *before*, *then*, *later*, *soon*, *next*, and *finally* give you clues to chronological order.

2. **Identify major events in the sequence.** You do not need to worry about minor events or details. Focusing on major events will help you understand their order.

3. **Put events in the correct order.** A sequence chain like the one here might help you organize information as you identify sequence.

Western Frontier

Most colonial settlements were located along the Atlantic coast. Colonial settlers, or pioneers, slowly moved into the Virginia and Carolina backcountry and the Ohio River valley.

Indian leaders like Chief Pontiac opposed British settlement of this new land. Pontiac's Rebellion began in May 1763 when his forces attacked British forts on the frontier. Within one month, they had destroyed or captured seven forts. Pontiac then led an attack on Fort Detroit. The British held out for months.

British leaders feared that more fighting would take place on the frontier if colonists kept moving onto American Indian lands. To avoid more conflict, King George III issued the Proclamation of 1763. This law banned British settlement west of the Appalachian Mountains. The law also ordered settlers to leave the upper Ohio River valley.

From *United States History*, The English Colonies

First
Pioneers began to establish new settlements on American Indian land.

Next
Pontiac's Rebellion begins when Chief Pontiac's forces attack British forts in May 1763.

Next
Pontiac attacks Fort Detroit, where the British hold out for months.

Last
King George III issues the Proclamation of 1763, banning British settlement in the west.

Sequencing

As you read about United States history you will come across a lot of new information. To understand how events unfolded, you need to be able to identify the order in which they happened—their sequence.

YOU TRY IT!

Read the following passage about the Allies' invasion of Italy. Create a sequence chain describing the major events of the invasion.

On to Italy

The first major step in this assault was the July 1943 invasion of the island of Sicily. Soon after the attack began, Roosevelt and Churchill issued a message to the Italian people asking them "whether they want to die for Mussolini and Hitler or live for Italy and civilization." The Italians chose life. By the end of the month, they had turned against dictator Benito Mussolini and forced him from power. The Allies took Sicily a few weeks later. They planned next to occupy the Italian Peninsula.

Hitler, however, was not going to let the Allies simply march through Italy and into Europe. German forces rushed to stop them.

Despite German resistance, the Allies made steady progress at first. Taking part in the fighting were the Tuskegee Airmen. This was a segregated unit of African Americans, the first ever to receive training as pilots in the U.S. military.

From *American Anthem*, The United States in World War II

First
_____
_____
_____
_____
_____

Next
_____
_____
_____
_____
_____

Next
_____
_____
_____
_____
_____

Last
_____
_____
_____
_____
_____

Sequencing

Reading World History

As you read about world history you will come across a lot of new information. To understand how events unfolded, you need to be able to identify the order in which they happened—their sequence.

YOU TRY IT!

Read the following passage about the Tokugawa shogunate. Create a sequence chain describing the major events in its rise to power in Japan.

Strong Leaders Take Over

Soon new leaders rose to power. They began as local rulers, but these men wanted more power. In the 1500s, each fought to unify all of Japan under his control.

The first such leader was Oda Nobunaga. Oda gave his soldiers guns that had been brought to Japan by Portuguese traders. This was the first time guns had been used in Japan. With these new weapons, Oda easily defeated his opponents.

After Oda died, other leaders continued his efforts to unify Japan. By 1600, one of them, Tokugawa Ieyasu, had conquered his enemies. In 1603 Japan's emperor made Tokugawa shogun. From his capital at Edo—now Tokyo—Tokugawa ruled all of Japan.

Tokugawa's rise to power began the Tokugawa shogunate, or rule by shoguns of the Tokugawa family. Early in this period, which lasted until 1868, Japan traded with other countries and let Christian missionaries live in Japan.

From *World History*, Japan

First
_____
_____
_____
_____

▼

Next
_____
_____
_____
_____

▼

Next
_____
_____
_____
_____

▼

Last
_____
_____
_____
_____

Thinking about Content Reading

Sequencing

As you read about geography you will come across a lot of new information. To understand how events unfolded, you need to be able to identify the order in which they happened—their sequence.

YOU TRY IT!

Read the following passage about the water cycle. Create a sequence chain describing the order of events as water changes form.

The Water Cycle

Water is always moving. As water heats up and cools down, it moves from the planet's surface to the atmosphere, or the mass of air that surrounds Earth. One of the most important processes in nature is the water cycle. The water cycle is the movement of water from Earth's surface to the atmosphere and back.

The sun's energy drives the water cycle. As the sun heats water on Earth's surface, some of that water evaporates, or turns from liquid to gas, or water vapor. Water vapor then rises into the air. As the vapor rises, it cools. The cooling causes the water vapor to condense, or change from a vapor into tiny liquid droplets. These droplets join together to form clouds. If the droplets become heavy enough, precipitation occurs—that is, the water falls back to Earth as rain, snow, sleet, or hail.

When that precipitation falls back to Earth's surface, some of the water is absorbed into the soil as groundwater. Excess water, called runoff, flows over land and collects in streams, rivers, and oceans. Because the water cycle is constantly repeating, it allows us to maintain a fairly constant supply of water on Earth.

From *Introduction to Geography*, Planet Earth

First

_____
_____
_____
_____
_____

▼

Next

_____
_____
_____
_____
_____

▼

Next

_____
_____
_____
_____
_____

▼

Last

_____
_____
_____
_____
_____

Sequencing

As you read about civics and government you will come across a lot of new information. To understand how events unfolded, you need to be able to identify the order in which they happened—their sequence.

YOU TRY IT!

Read the following passage about the Supreme Court. Create a sequence chain describing how the Court makes decisions.

Hearing and Deciding Cases

The Supreme Court hears cases by oral argument. Lawyers for the parties in a case each have 30 minutes to present their arguments. Then the justices spend their time reading written arguments and considering what was said in court. When they are ready to decide a case, they hold a private meeting to vote. Each justice has one vote, and decisions are reached by a simple majority.

Eventually, the justices inform the parties of the court's opinion. An opinion explains the reasoning that led to the decision. The Supreme Court's opinion is binding on all lower courts. Sometimes a justice agrees with the decision of the majority, but for different reasons. In that case, the justice may decide to write a concurring opinion.

In many cases, one or more justices disagree with the majority opinion. These justices may file a dissenting opinion. The dissenting opinion explains why the justice believes the majority opinion is wrong. Although dissenting opinions have no effect on the law, they are still important. Many dissenting opinions have later become the law of the land when the beliefs of society and the opinions of the justices change.

From *Civics in Practice*, The Judicial Branch

First
_____
_____
_____
_____

▼

Next
_____
_____
_____
_____

▼

Next
_____
_____
_____
_____

▼

Last
_____
_____
_____
_____
_____

Sequencing

As you read about economics you will come across a lot of new information. To understand how events unfolded, you need to be able to identify the order in which they happened—their sequence.

YOU TRY IT!

Read the following passage about the First Bank of the United States. Create a sequence chain describing important events related to the First Bank of the United States.

First Bank of the United States

In 1791 Congress established the First Bank of the United States as a private business. Its 20-year charter, or legal permission to operate, outlined the First Bank's responsibilities, which included the issuing of representative money in the form of banknotes. Additionally, the First Bank collected fees and made payments for the federal government.

One year later in 1792 Congress established a national coinage system, and the federal government began to mint gold and silver coins. The government also established the dollar as the official unit of currency.

How successful was the First Bank? It did bring some order to the monetary and banking systems in the United States. It also was successful in regulating banks chartered by the states. For example, the First Bank of the United States required state-chartered banks to hold gold and silver that could be exchanged for currency. Nonetheless, congressional opponents of the First Bank succeeded in voting down the renewal of its 20-year charter in 1811.

From *Holt Economics*, Money and the Banking System

First
_____
_____
_____
_____
_____

▼

Next
_____
_____
_____
_____
_____

▼

Next
_____
_____
_____
_____
_____

▼

Last
_____
_____
_____
_____
_____

Maybe you have heard this old riddle: "Which came first, the chicken or the egg?" The riddle is asking if the chicken is a cause or an effect. If the chicken came first, the chicken is a cause. If the egg came first, though, the chicken is an effect. What makes the riddle fun is that both the chicken and the egg could be a cause and an effect.

As you read social studies it is important to identify causes and effects. A cause makes something happen. An effect is what happens as a result of a cause.

HOW TO IDENTIFY CAUSE AND EFFECT

To identify causes and effects, follow these three basic steps:

1. Look for key words that signal cause. Words such as *reason, basis, because,* and *as* are often used in a discussion of causes. Sometimes a cause is only implied.

2. Look for key words that signal effect. Words and phrases such as *therefore, so, as a result,* and *for that reason* are often used to describe effects.

3. Check to see if there are multiple causes and effects. Sometimes one cause will create many effects. Other times one effect will have many causes. It is also possible for a cause to lead to an effect, which is in turn a cause of another effect.

The Monarchy Ends

In 1791, the National Assembly finally completed its constitution. It created a new legislative body, the Legislative Assembly. The constitution allowed the French monarchy to continue, but with severe restrictions on the king's power.

With this development, the king and queen suspected that they were not safe. In June 1791 they disguised themselves and tried to flee Paris. They were recognized, however, and rushed back to the Tuileries palace.

From *World History*, The French Revolution and Napoleon

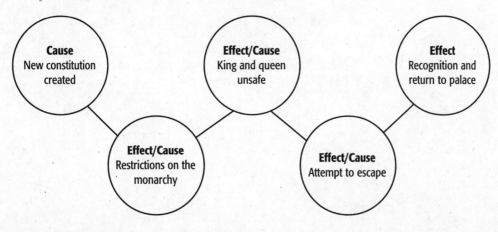

Identifying Cause and Effect

As you read about United States history you will come across a lot of new information. You will understand United States history better if you learn to recognize causes and effects.

YOU TRY IT!

Read the following passage about changes in the economy. Then fill in the diagram with causes and effect discussed.

Weaknesses in the Economy

In Florida the wild land boom came to a sudden and disastrous end. Demand for land peaked, then collapsed. Then came "The Big Blow"—the strongest hurricane recorded up to that time. The hurricane had winds of 150 miles per hour, and it killed 243 people. Few people heard the warning on South Florida's only radio station. The hurricane was one of the most destructive ever. As a result, Florida sunk into an economic depression even as other parts of the nation enjoyed prosperity.

From *American Anthem*, From War to Peace

Cause and Effect Chain

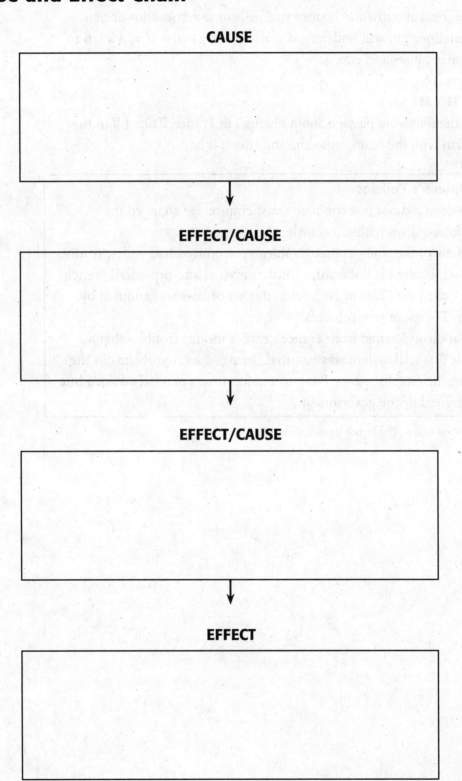

CAUSE

EFFECT/CAUSE

EFFECT/CAUSE

EFFECT

Name _____ Class _____ Date _____

Identifying Cause and Effect

Reading Skills

Reading World History

As you read about world history you will come across a lot of new information. You will understand world history better if you learn to recognize causes and effects.

YOU TRY IT!
Read the following passage about changes in France. Then fill in the diagram with the main cause and the effects it had.

Napoleon's Policies

Napoleon did not just conquer a vast empire. He changed the millions of lives within its borders in several ways.

Many of the changes that Napoleon introduced had widespread impact. Under his leadership, scholars revised and organized French law. Called the Code of Napoleon, this set of laws was adopted by many European governments.

Napoleon learned from France's earlier money troubles that a stable financial system was essential. To avoid such problems in the future, he established the Bank of France. It was privately owned but supervised by the government.

From *World History*, The French Revolution and Napoleon

Thinking about Content Reading

Cause and Effect Chain

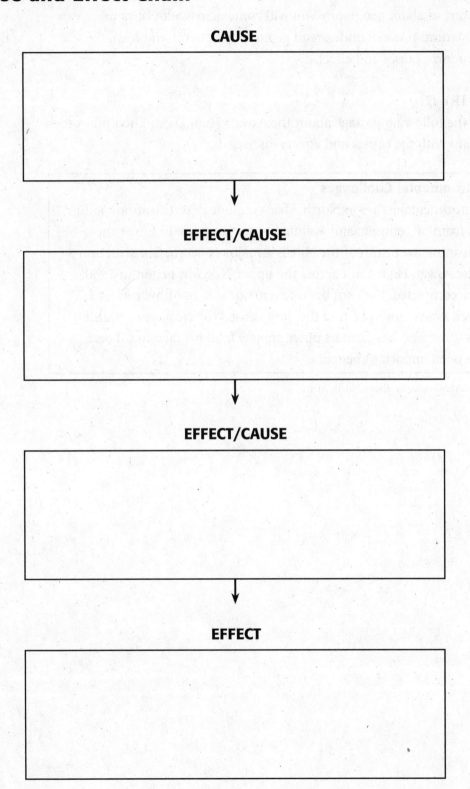

CAUSE

EFFECT/CAUSE

EFFECT/CAUSE

EFFECT

Identifying Cause and Effect

As you read about geography you will come across a lot of new information. You will understand geography better if you learn to recognize causes and effects.

YOU TRY IT!

Read the following passage about the Aswan High Dam. Then fill in the diagram with the causes and effects discussed.

Environmental Challenges

Environmental issues in North Africa include desertification, pollution from oil refining, and polluted water supplies. In Egypt the environmental health of the Nile is a major concern. Construction of the Aswan High Dam across the upper Nile was begun in 1960. Once completed, the dam became a major source of hydroelectric power. Water stored behind the dam is used for crops year-round. This water also lets farmers open up new land for farming. These have been important benefits.

From *World Geography Today*, North Africa

Cause and Effect Chain

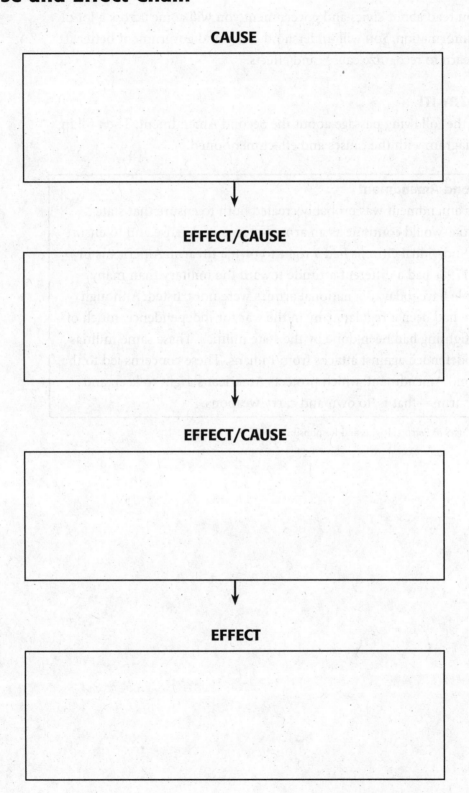

CAUSE

EFFECT/CAUSE

EFFECT/CAUSE

EFFECT

Identifying Cause and Effect

As you read about civics and government you will come across a lot of new information. You will understand civics and government better if you learn to recognize causes and effects.

YOU TRY IT!

Read the following passage about the Second Amendment. Then fill in the diagram with the causes and effect mentioned.

Second Amendment

This amendment was probably created both to ensure that state militias would continue as an armed means of defense and to ensure that individual citizens had a right to own a firearm. Americans in the 1790s had a different attitude toward the military than many people have today. Big national armies were not trusted. Although there had been a regular army in the war for independence, much of the fighting had been done by the state militias. These same militias also defended against attacks from Indians. These concerns led to the Second Amendment, which protects Americans' right to keep and bear arms—that is, to own and carry weapons.

From *Civics in Practice*, Rights and Responsibilities

Thinking about Content Reading

Cause and Effect Chain

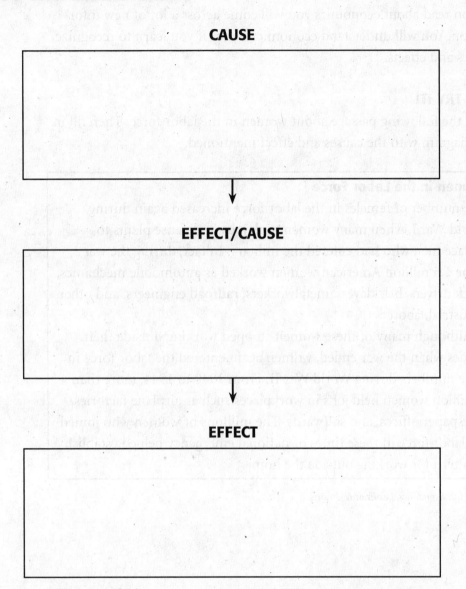

CAUSE

EFFECT/CAUSE

EFFECT

Identifying Cause and Effect

As you read about economics you will come across a lot of new information. You will understand economics better if you learn to recognize causes and effects.

YOU TRY IT!
Read the following passage about women in the labor force. Then fill in the diagram with the causes and effect mentioned.

Women in the Labor Force

The number of females in the labor force increased again during World War I, when many women took jobs in defense plants to replace men who had entered the military. In fact, during the war some 1.5 million American women worked as automobile mechanics, truck drivers, bricklayers, metalworkers, railroad engineers, and other industrial laborers.

Although many of these women stopped working outside their homes when the war ended, women again entered the labor force in large numbers during World War II. From 1940 to 1944, more than 4 million women held jobs in workplaces such as airplane factories, newspaper offices, and shipyards. The millions of women who joined the labor force in these times of national emergency helped establish a pattern for working outside the home.

From *Holt Economics*, Labor and Unions

Thinking about Content Reading

Cause and Effect Chain

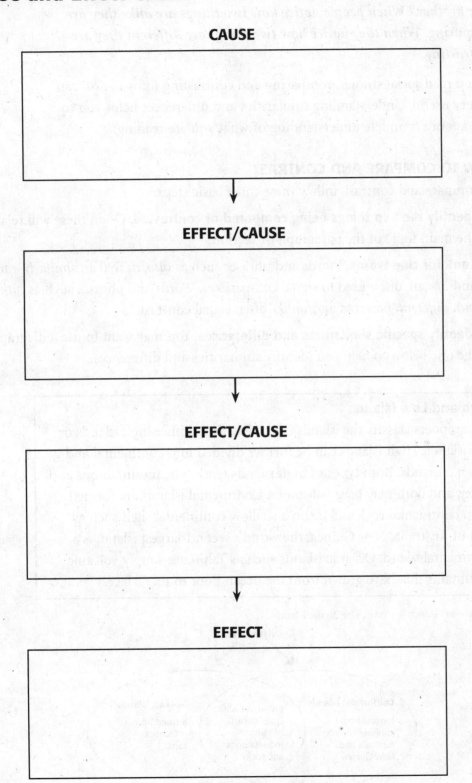

CAUSE

EFFECT/CAUSE

EFFECT/CAUSE

EFFECT

If you have a brother or a sister, you might be used to hearing things like this: "You are so different from your sister," or "You look just like your brother." When people notice how two things are alike they are comparing. When they notice how two things are different they are contrasting.

As you read social studies, comparing and contrasting information can be very useful. Understanding similarities and differences helps you to gain a more complete understanding of what you are reading.

HOW TO COMPARE AND CONTRAST

To compare and contrast, follow these three basic steps:

1. **Identify the two things being compared or contrasted.** Often these will relate to the main topic of the paragraph or section.

2. **Look for clue words.** Words and phrases such as *also, as well as, similarly, same,* and *like* are often used to signal comparison. Words and phrases such as *although, but, different, however,* and *unlike* often signal contrast.

3. **Identify specific similarities and differences.** You may want to use a diagram like the one below to help you identify similarities and differences.

High and Low Islands

Geographers classify the islands of the Pacific as either high islands or low islands. High islands can be further divided into continental and oceanic islands. Both types of high islands tend to be mountainous and rocky, and both may have volcanoes. Continental islands are formed from continental rock and lie on a shallow continental shelf such as that of Australia. New Guinea, the world's second-largest island, is a continental island. Oceanic islands such as Tahiti are simply volcanic mountains that have grown from the ocean floor to its surface.

From *World Geography Today*, The Pacific Islands

Name _____ Class _____ Date _____

Comparing and Contrasting

As you read about United States history you will come across a lot of new information. You will understand United States history better if you learn to compare and contrast information.

YOU TRY IT!

Read the following passage about presidents Roosevelt and Taft. Then fill in the diagram with their similarities and differences.

Progressivism under Taft

Theodore Roosevelt hoped that his secretary of war, William Howard Taft, would take his place as president in 1908. Like Roosevelt, Taft favored business regulation and opposed socialism. With Roosevelt's assistance, Taft defeated William Jennings Bryan in the election of 1908.

   Despite their friendship, Roosevelt and Taft held different ideas about how a president should act. Taft thought Roosevelt had claimed more power than a president was constitutionally allowed.

   As president, therefore, Taft chose to move cautiously toward reform and regulation. This upset Roosevelt and various Progressives, who supported stricter regulation of big business. Although Taft's administration started twice as many antitrust lawsuits as Roosevelt's had, Progressives were not satisfied.

From *American Anthem*, The Progressives

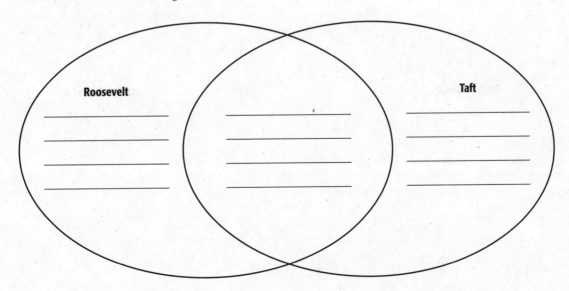

Thinking about Content Reading

Name _____ Class _____ Date _____

Comparing and Contrasting

As you read about world history you will come across a lot of new information. You will understand world history better if you learn to compare and contrast information.

YOU TRY IT!

Read the following passage about ancient democracy in Greece and modern democracy in the United States. Then fill in the diagram with their similarities and differences.

Ancient Democracy Differs from Modern Democracy

Like ancient Athens, the Unites States has a democratic government in which the people hold power. But our modern democracy is very different from the ancient Athenians' democracy.

All citizens in Athens could participate directly in the government. We call this form of government a direct democracy. It is called direct democracy because each person's decision directly affects the outcome of a vote. In Athens, citizens gathered together to discuss issues and vote on them. Each person's vote counted, and the majority ruled.

The United States is too large for direct democracy to work for the whole country. For example, it would be impossible for all citizens to gather in one place for a debate. Instead, the founders of the United States set up another kind of democracy.

From *World History*, Ancient Greece

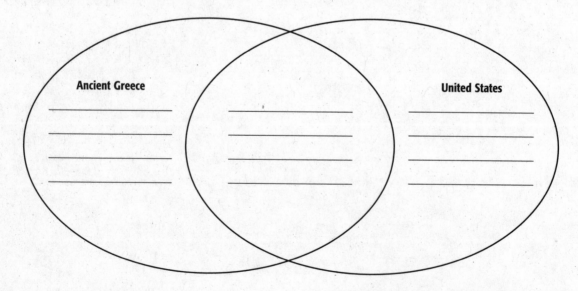

Comparing and Contrasting

Reading Skills
Reading Geography

As you read about geography you will come across a lot of new information. You will understand geography better if you learn to compare and contrast information.

YOU TRY IT!
Read the following passage about the Rhine and Danube rivers. Then fill in the diagram with their similarities and differences.

Water

The Rhine and Danube stand out among Europe's most important rivers. Many cities and industrial areas line their banks, and barges carry goods along their courses. The Rhine rises in the Swiss Alps. It then flows northwestward through Germany and the Netherlands before entering the North Sea. The Danube begins in the uplands of southern Germany. It flows eastward through nine countries in central and eastern Europe. It empties into the Black Sea. Unfortunately, large amounts of pollution enter the ocean from these and other rivers. Cleaning up and controlling pollution in Europe's rivers is a major environmental challenge.

From *World Geography Today*, Natural Environments of Europe

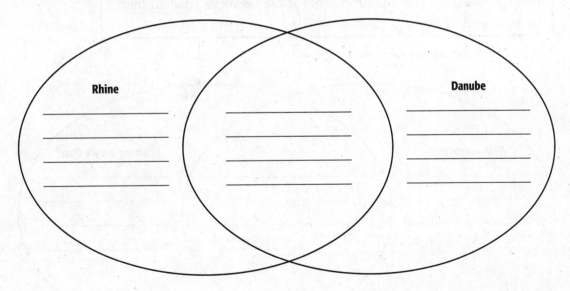

Thinking about Content Reading

Comparing and Contrasting

As you read about civics and government you will come across a lot of new information. You will understand civics and government better if you learn to compare and contrast information.

YOU TRY IT!
Read the following passage about different forms of city government. Then fill in the diagram with their similarities and differences.

Forms of City Government
Under the weak-mayor plan, the city council holds more power than the mayor. For example, the council appoints the city department heads, who report directly to the city council rather than to the mayor. The weak-mayor plan often results in conflicts between the council and the mayor.

Recently, many city governments using the mayor-council form of government have adopted a strong-mayor plan of city government. Under the strong-mayor plan, the mayor is the city's chief executive officer and has the primary responsibility for running the city's government. For example, the mayor appoints most of the city officials . . . Because executive power is concentrated in the mayor, many people think that the strong-mayor plan is more efficient than the weak-mayor form.

From *Civics in Practice*, Local Government

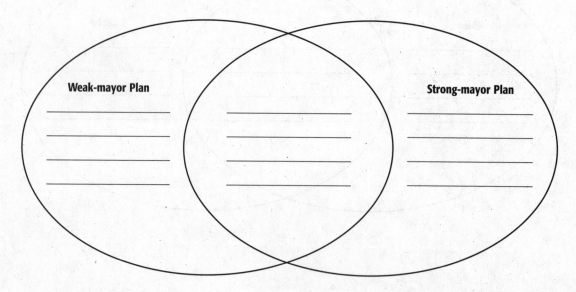

Comparing and Contrasting

Reading Skills

Reading Economics

As you read about economics you will come across a lot of new information. You will understand economics better if you learn to compare and contrast information.

YOU TRY IT!

Read the following passage about monopolistic competition. Then fill in the diagram to show the similarities and differences between monopolistic competition and perfect competition.

Monopolistic Competition

Monopolistic competition differs from perfect competition in one key respect—sellers offer different, rather than identical, products. Each firm seeks to have monopoly-like power by selling a unique product. Product variation is much more common than having identical products. As a result, monopolistic competition is much more common than perfect competition.

There are, however, similarities between the two systems. First, both buyers and sellers in monopolistic competition compete under the laws of supply and demand, just as they do in perfect competition. In addition, both systems feature many buyers and sellers acting independently, buyers who are well informed about products, and ease of market entry or exit.

From *Holt Economics*, Market Structures

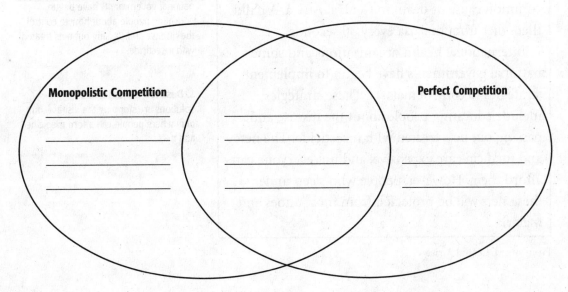

Maybe you have heard the common saying, "When life gives you lemons, make lemonade." In other words, when life gives you a problem, work to find a good solution.

As you read social studies, you will learn about how different people and countries have solved problems. Learning to identify these problems and their solutions as you read will help you understand the information better.

HOW TO IDENTIFY PROBLEMS AND SOLUTIONS

To identify problems and solutions, follow these three basic steps:

1. **Recognize the problem.** Anytime you read about a conflict, crisis, or need, you are reading about a problem. Make sure you know exactly what the problem is, whom it affects, and why it is a problem.

2. **Look for the solution.** Sometimes only one solution is discussed in the text. Other times, you may read about several solutions to the same problem.

3. **Describe the outcome.** Did an attempted solution solve the problem? Or did it fail? Sometimes the text will describe and evaluate the outcome of the solution. Other times, you should try to evaluate on your own whether or not the solution was a good one.

Health

Like war, disease kills many people in the region. Malaria is a disease spread by mosquitoes that causes fever and pain. Without treatment it can lead to death. In fact, malaria is by far the most common cause of death in Central Africa. A child there dies from malaria every 30 seconds . . .

International health organizations and some national governments have begun to implement strategies to control malaria. These strategies include educating people about the disease and passing out nets treated with insecticide. The nets and medicine are expensive, and not everyone can afford them. However, people who sleep under these nets will be protected from mosquitoes and malaria.

From *Africa*, Central Africa

1. Recognize a problem.
Malaria, a disease spread by mosquitoes, kills many people in Central Africa.

2. Look for the solution.
International health organizations and national governments have begun educating people about how to control the disease and passing out nets treated with insecticide.

3. Describe the outcome.
Solutions are stopping the disease, but only where people can afford medicine and nets.

Thinking about Content Reading

Identifying Problems and Solutions

Reading Skills

Reading United States History

As you read about United States history you will come across a lot of new information: Sometimes you will read about problems people and countries have faced. Identifying these problems and their solutions will help you get a better understanding of history.

YOU TRY IT!

Read the following passage. Then complete the graphic organizer to help you identify a problem, its solution, and the outcome.

Inflation and Price Controls

A particular worry was the high rate of inflation, or the overall rise in prices. In the months leading up to the 1972 election, this stood at an unacceptable five percent, and it was rising. Unemployment was also at an uncomfortably high level.

Nixon had traditionally favored limited government involvement in the economy. Now, however, he was willing to take action. In August 1971, he announced a 90-day freeze in wages and prices. That is, businesses could not increase the prices they charged for their products or the wages they paid their workers. This, Nixon hoped, would act as a brake on inflation.

The immediate impact of Nixon's measures was positive. Inflation did appear to slow, at least for a while. Nixon seemed to have successfully addressed a major economic concern of the voters.

Unfortunately, Nixon had not solved the problem of inflation permanently. The oil crisis of 1973–1974 would soon send prices sharply higher again. The wage and price controls that had worked in 1971 failed to bring relief.

From *American Anthem*, A Search for Order

Problem

_____
_____
_____
_____
_____
_____
_____

▼

Solution

_____
_____
_____
_____
_____
_____

▼

Outcome

_____
_____
_____
_____
_____
_____
_____
_____
_____

Identifying Problems and Solutions

Reading Skills
Reading World History

As you read about world history you will come across a lot of new information. Sometimes you will read about problems people and countries have faced. Identifying these problems and their solutions will help you get a better understanding of history.

YOU TRY IT!

Read the following passage. Then complete the graphic organizer to help you identify a problem, its solution, and the outcome.

Written Laws Keep Order

Rome's officials were responsible for making the city's laws and making sure that people followed them. At first these laws weren't written down. The only people who knew all the laws were the patricians who had made them.

Many people were unhappy with this situation. They did not want to be punished for breaking laws they didn't even know existed. As a result, they began to call for Rome's laws to be written down and made accessible to everybody.

Rome's first written law code was produced in 450 BC on 12 bronze tables, or tablets. These tables were displayed in the Forum, Rome's public meeting place. Because of how it was displayed, this code was called the Law of the Twelve Tables.

Over time, Rome's leaders passed many new laws. Throughout their history, though, the Romans looked to the Law of the Twelve Tables as a symbol of Roman law and of their rights as Roman citizens.

From *World History*, The Roman Republic

Problem
_____
_____
_____
_____
_____
_____

▼

Solution
_____
_____
_____
_____
_____
_____

▼

Outcome
_____
_____
_____
_____
_____
_____
_____
_____

Identifying Problems and Solutions

As you read about geography you will come across a lot of new information. Sometimes you will read about problems people and countries have faced. Identifying these problems and their solutions will help you get a better understanding of geography.

YOU TRY IT!

Read the following passage. Then complete the graphic organizer to help you identify a problem, its solution, and the outcome.

The Region Today

Estonia, Latvia, Lithuania, and Poland all still feel the effects of decades of Soviet rule. The economies of all four countries suffered because the Soviets did not build a decent infrastructure. An infrastructure is the set of resources, like roads, airports, and factories, that a country needs in order to support economic activities. The many factories built by the Soviets in Poland and the Baltics could not produce as many goods as those in Western Europe.

Today Poland and the Baltic Republics are working to rebuild and strengthen their economies. They are replacing the old and outdated factories built by the Soviets with new ones that take advantage of modern technology. As a result, cities like Warsaw, the capital of Poland, have become major industrial centers.

To further their economic growth, the countries of this region are also seeking new sources of income. One area in which they have found some success is tourism. Since the collapse of the Soviet Union in 1991, many Americans and Western Europeans have begun visiting. Polish cities like Warsaw and Krakow have long attracted tourists with their rich history and famous sites.

From *Europe and Russia*, Eastern Europe

Problem
_____
_____
_____
_____
_____
_____

▼

Solution
_____
_____
_____
_____
_____
_____

▼

Outcome
_____
_____
_____
_____
_____
_____
_____

Identifying Problems and Solutions

Reading Skills
Reading Civics

As you read about civics and government you will come across a lot of new information. Sometimes you will read about problems people and countries have faced. Identifying these problems and their solutions will help you get a better understanding of government.

YOU TRY IT!

Read the following passage. Then complete the graphic organizer to help you identify a problem, its solution, and the outcome.

Writing the Constitution

The delegates discussed many ideas and proposals for organizing the federal system. They eventually settled many differences of opinion by a series of compromises. A compromise is an agreement in which each side gives up part of its demands in order to reach a solution to a problem.

The most serious disagreement arose over the question of representation in the new national legislature, or lawmaking body. The larger states favored a legislature in which representation would be based on the size of a state's population. The smaller states wanted each state to have an equal number of representatives in the legislature.

Finally, both sides agreed to a compromise. Their agreement provided for a bicameral law-making body called Congress. In one house, the Senate, the states were to have equal representation. In the other house, the House of Representatives, each state was to be represented according to the size of its population. This agreement became known as the Great Compromise.

From *Civics in Practice*, Foundations of Government

Problem
_____
_____
_____
_____
_____
_____
_____

▼

Solution
_____
_____
_____
_____
_____
_____
_____

▼

Outcome
_____
_____
_____
_____
_____
_____
_____
_____

Identifying Problems and Solutions

Reading Skills
Reading Economics

As you read about economics you will come across a lot of new information. Sometimes you will read about economic problems people and countries have faced. Identifying these problems and their solutions will help you get a better understanding of economics.

YOU TRY IT!

Read the following passage. Then complete the graphic organizer to help you identify a problem, its solution, and the outcome.

New Deal Banking Reform

The Great Depression was brought on by a financial panic that swept the nation. Thousands of people withdrew their savings, causing many banks to fail. In the years 1930–33, nearly 8,000 banks went under, some 4,000 in 1933 alone.

Franklin D. Roosevelt's election to the presidency in 1932 brought lasting changes to the monetary and banking systems. Promising a "New Deal" to the nation's people, Roosevelt sought to restore public confidence in the economy and the nation's banking system.

For example, Roosevelt kept the nation's banks closed for four days in March 1933. The president's order for the "bank holiday" allowed banks to reopen only after federal auditors judged them to be financially sound. Most banks were reopened within two weeks. Certification by the auditors helped restore confidence in the reopened banks, and soon people and businesses began to use the banks again.

From *Holt Economics*, Money and the Banking System

Problem
_____
_____
_____
_____
_____
_____
_____

▼

Solution
_____
_____
_____
_____
_____
_____
_____

▼

Outcome
_____
_____
_____
_____
_____
_____
_____

Have you ever read a mystery story in which a detective puts together various clues to solve a puzzling crime? In other words, the detective combines various bits of information to reach a conclusion.

A conclusion is a judgment someone makes by combining information. When you read, you can put together various bits of information from what you are reading to figure out new information that is not exactly stated in the text. Drawing conclusions will make you a better reader.

HOW TO DRAW CONCLUSIONS

To draw conclusions, follow these three basic steps:

1. **Read the text to understand the topic.** It is a good idea to read the text looking for clues, even if you do not know yet where they will lead you.

2. **Ask a question that the text does not directly answer.** After you have read the text, think of a question that is related to the information but not directly answered in the text.

3. **Put together clues, or information in the text, to answer the question.** Think back over the information in the text to see if it leads you to discover, or draw a conclusion about, the answer to your question.

The Pyramids

Egyptians believed that burial sites, especially royal tombs, were very important. As a result, they built spectacular monuments in which to bury their rulers. The most spectacular of all were the pyramids, huge stone tombs with four triangle-shaped walls that met in a point on top.

The Egyptians began to build pyramids during the Old Kingdom. Some of the largest pyramids ever constructed were built during this time. Many of these huge structures are still standing. The largest is the Great Pyramid of Khufu near the town of Giza. It covers more than 13 acres at its base and stands 481 feet high. This single pyramid took more than 2 million limestone blocks to build.

From *World History*, Ancient Egypt and Kush

Question
Who was Khufu?

▼

Information from the text
- Egyptians built spectacular monuments in which to bury their rulers.
- The pyramids were tombs.
- The largest pyramid is named after Khufu.

▼

Conclusion
Khufu was an important ruler of Egypt.

Drawing Conclusions

Reading Skills

Reading United States History

As you read about United States history you will come across a lot of new information. Drawing conclusions helps you put together information to get a more complete understanding of the text.

YOU TRY IT!

Read the following passage. Then put together information from the passage to draw a conclusion about the question in the graphic organizer.

Maryland

In 1634 a group of 200 English Catholics came to Maryland. Included in the group were wealthy landowners, servants, craftspeople, and farmers. Settlers in Maryland benefited from the lessons learned by the Jamestown colonists. They spent their time raising corn, cattle, and hogs so that they would have enough to eat. Before long, many colonists also began growing tobacco for profit.

Although Catholics founded Maryland, a growing number of Protestants began moving there in the 1640s. Soon, religious conflicts arose between Catholics and Protestants in the colony. To reduce tensions, Lord Baltimore presented a bill to the colonial assembly that became known as the Toleration Act of 1649. This bill made it a crime to restrict the religious rights of Christians. This was the first law supporting religious tolerance passed in the English colonies.

From *United States History*, The English Colonies

Question
What was Lord Baltimore's view of religion?

▼

Information from the text
_____
_____
_____
_____
_____
_____
_____
_____

▼

Conclusion
_____
_____
_____
_____
_____
_____
_____

Drawing Conclusions

As you read about world history you will come across a lot of new information. Drawing conclusions helps you put together information to get a more complete understanding of the text.

YOU TRY IT!

Read the following passage. Then put together information from the passage to draw a conclusion about the question in the graphic organizer.

The Revival of the Family

Since Confucianism was the official government philosophy during Wudi's reign, Confucian teachings about the family were also honored. Children were taught from birth to respect their elders. Disobeying one's parents was a crime. Even emperors had a duty to respect their parents.

Confucius had taught that the father was the head of the family. Within the family, the father had absolute power. The Han taught that it was a woman's duty to obey her husband, and children had to obey their father.

Han officials believed that if the family was strong and people obeyed the father, then people would obey the emperor, too. Since the Han stressed strong family ties and respect for elders, some men even gained government jobs based on the respect they showed their parents.

Children were encouraged to serve their parents. They were also expected to honor dead parents with ceremonies and offerings. All family members were expected to care for family burial sites.

From *World History*, Ancient China

Question
How did the ancient Chinese view Emperor Wudi?

▼

Information from the text

_____
_____
_____
_____
_____
_____
_____
_____

▼

Conclusion

_____
_____
_____
_____
_____
_____

Thinking about Content Reading

Drawing Conclusions

As you read about geography you will come across a lot of new information. Drawing conclusions helps you put together information to get a more complete understanding of the text.

YOU TRY IT!

Read the following passage. Then put together information from the passage to draw a conclusion about the question in the graphic organizer.

Water

The main water sources in southern Central Asia are the Syr Darya and Amu Darya rivers. Since water is so scarce there, different ideas over how to use the water from these rivers have led to conflict between Uzbekistan and Turkmenistan.

Today farmers use river water mostly to irrigate cotton fields. Cotton grows well in Central Asia's sunny climate, but it requires a lot of water. Irrigation has taken so much water from the rivers that almost no water actually reaches the Aral Sea today. The effect of this irrigation has been devastating to the Aral Sea. It has lost more than 75 percent of its water since 1960. Large areas of seafloor are now exposed.

In addition to water for irrigation, Central Asia's rivers supply power. Some countries have built large dams on the rivers to generate hydroelectricity.

From *Southwest and Central Asia*, Central Asia

Question
What different views might people in Uzbekistan and Turkmenistan have about the use of water from the Syr Darya and Amu Darya?

▼

Information from the text
_____
_____
_____
_____
_____
_____
_____
_____
_____
_____

▼

Conclusion
_____
_____
_____
_____
_____
_____

Thinking about Content Reading

Drawing Conclusions   Reading Skills

                                            Reading Civics

As you read about civics and government you will come across a lot of new information. Drawing conclusions helps you put together information to get a more complete understanding of the text.

YOU TRY IT!

Read the following passage. Then put together information from the passage to draw a conclusion about the question in the graphic organizer.

Import Taxes

The U.S. government collects taxes on many products imported from foreign countries. This import tax is called a tariff, or sometimes a customs duty. At one time customs duties were the main source of revenues for the federal government. For example, in 1850 about 90 percent of the federal budget came from customs duties.

Today the United States uses tariffs primarily to regulate foreign trade rather than to raise money. For example, tariffs can be used to raise the prices of imported goods. Tariffs make goods from other countries either as expensive or more expensive than American-made products. In this way tariffs can protect American industry from unfair competition from foreign industry. On the other hand, tariffs can also hurt American consumers by raising the prices of certain products. Using tariffs as a way to control trade, rather than as a source of revenue, is often a difficult balancing act.

From *Civics in Practice*, Paying for Government

Question
What would happen if the government drastically lowered tariffs?

▼

Information from the text
_____
_____
_____
_____
_____
_____
_____
_____
_____
_____

▼

Conclusion
_____
_____
_____
_____
_____
_____
_____

Drawing Conclusions

As you read about economics you will come across a lot of new information. Drawing conclusions helps you put together information to get a more complete understanding of the text.

YOU TRY IT!

Read the following passage. Then put together information from the passage to draw a conclusion about the question in the graphic organizer.

Technology

Usually, new technology makes production more efficient and less expensive. This causes the costs of production to decrease. In turn, producers are able to supply more goods and services at each and every price because their costs are lower and their profits are higher.

Consider the case of automobiles. The first cars were produced individually by several workers. Because each car was made up of thousands of parts, production was time consuming and expensive. In the early 1900s, however, technology revolutionized automobile production. Around 1913 Henry Ford used a new production technique—the assembly line—to make cars in his Detroit-area factory. Car frames moved along a conveyor belt past workers who performed their specified tasks in the assembly process. New machines produced the individual automobile parts, which were carried to workers on the assembly line.

The new technology had dramatic results. Assembly time was reduced significantly for Ford's Model T automobile. For the same amount of time and money as before, Ford's company could now produce many more Model T automobiles.

From *Holt Economics*, Supply

Question
How did a change in technology benefit Henry Ford's company and consumers?

▼

Information from the text
_____
_____
_____
_____
_____
_____
_____
_____
_____
_____

▼

Conclusion
_____
_____
_____
_____
_____
_____
_____

Thinking about Content Reading

Maybe you have heard someone say, "Girls like dolls," or "Boys like trucks." What do you think of those statements? They are probably true in general, but they are not true for all girls and boys, or course. Statements like those are called generalizations.

A generalization is a broad, general conclusion drawn from several examples or pieces of evidence. As you read social studies, practice making generalizations about the text. Doing so will help you focus on the main points of your reading.

HOW TO MAKE GENERALIZATIONS

To make generalizations, follow these three basic steps:

1. **Note details or examples related to a particular topic in the text.** Often an author will provide several examples to make a main point.

2. **Make a broad statement based on examples or evidence.** Information in the text should lead you to a general conclusion about the topic.

3. **Check that your generalization is valid.** Your statement should allow for exceptions. Some words you can use to show there may be exceptions to your statement are *most, some, often,* and *generally.* Watch out for generalizations that try to apply one idea to every person or situation.

Finding Work

Immigrants with skills that were in demand sometimes found work outside factories and sweatshops. For example, some immigrants worked as bakers, carpenters, masons, or skilled machinists. Others saved or borrowed money to open small businesses such as laundries, barbershops, or street vending carts. New immigrants often opened the same types of businesses in which other immigrants from the same country were already succeeding. They worked hard for long hours to become successful themselves.

From *United States History*, Immigrants and Urban Life

Details or examples from the text
- Skilled immigrants found work in many industries.
- Immigrants opened small businesses.
- New immigrants worked hard for long hours.

Generalization
Immigrants contributed to the economy in many ways.

Making Generalizations

Reading Skills

Reading United States History

As you read about United States history you will come across a lot of new information. Making generalizations will help you sort through the details and focus on the main points of the text.

YOU TRY IT!

Read the following passage. Then use the graphic organizer below to make a generalization. Be sure to check that your generalization is valid and applies to different situations.

Cold War Policies

The United States quickly developed a new foreign policy to deal with the Cold War. It was based on the goal of containment, or preventing the Soviet Union from expanding its influence around the world.

In 1945 the Soviet Union began demanding control over areas in the Mediterranean Sea that were under Turkish authority. In 1946 Communist rebels in Greece threatened to topple the Greek monarchy. At Truman's request, Congress passed an aid package worth millions of dollars for Greece and Turkey. The money, the president said, would "support free peoples who are resisting attempted subjugation [conquest] by armed minorities or outside pressures." U.S. aid helped the Greek army defeat the Communist rebels and protected Turkey from Soviet expansion. This policy of providing aid to help foreign countries fight communism became known as the Truman Doctrine.

From *United States History*, Early Years of the Cold War

Details or examples from the text	Generalization
_____	_____
_____	_____
_____	_____
_____	_____
_____	_____
_____	_____
_____	_____
_____	_____
_____	_____

Making Generalizations

Reading Skills

Reading World History

As you read about world history you will come across a lot of new information. Making generalizations will help you sort through the details and focus on the main points of the text.

YOU TRY IT!

Read the following passage. Then use the graphic organizer below to make a generalization. Be sure to check that your generalization is valid and applies to different situations.

Napoleon's Rise to Power

By the summer of 1793, Robespierre and the Jacobins ruled France. Their control was incomplete, however. For example, royalists had let British troops occupy the port city of Toulon. Robespierre sent young Captain Napoleon Bonaparte to remove the royalists and their British supporters. He succeeded within 48 hours.

A year later, Bonaparte had another dazzling victory in Italy over Austrian troops. Then in 1795 he again faced off against rebellious French citizens. A mob was charging the Tuileries palace, so Bonaparte used artillery to shoot into the crowd. Some 200 people were killed, but the survivors fled. Bonaparte, now a general, was put in charge of defending the French interior. He was only 26 years old.

The young general continued to win battles against Italian and Austrian troops and to claim territory for France. He was a brilliant strategist, and his troops could strike quickly because they did not travel with a big supply train. Instead, they took the food they needed from the countryside.

From *World History*, The French Revolution and Napoleon

Details or examples from the text	Generalization
_____	_____
_____	_____
_____	_____
_____	_____
_____	_____
_____	_____
_____	_____

Making Generalizations

As you read about geography you will come across a lot of new information. Making generalizations will help you sort through the details and focus on the main points of the text.

YOU TRY IT!

Read the following passage. Then use the graphic organizer below to make a generalization. Be sure to check that your generalization is valid and applies to different situations.

Greater Mexico City

Greater Mexico City includes the capital and about 50 smaller cities near it. With a population of more than 19 million, Mexico City is the world's second-largest city and one of the most densely populated urban areas. Thousands of people move there every year looking for work.

While this region does provide job and educational opportunities not so easily found in the rest of the country, its huge population causes problems. For example, Mexico City is very polluted. Factories and cars release exhaust and other pollutants into the air. The surrounding mountains trap the resulting smog—a mixture of smoke, chemicals, and fog. Smog can cause health problems like eye irritation and breathing difficulties.

Another problem that comes from crowding is poverty. Wealth and poverty exist side by side in Mexico City. The city has large urban slums. The slums often exist right next to modern office building, apartments, museums, or universities.

From *The Americas*, Mexico

Details or examples from the text	Generalization
_____	_____
_____	_____
_____	_____
_____	_____
_____	_____
_____	_____
_____	_____

Making Generalizations

Reading Skills
Reading Civics

As you read about civics and government you will come across a lot of new information. Making generalizations will help you sort through the details and focus on the main points of the text.

YOU TRY IT!

Read the following passage. Then use the graphic organizer below to make a generalization. Be sure to check that your generalization is valid and applies to different situations.

Private Financing

Voters, business groups, labor unions, and many other organizations contribute money to the political party that they believe best represents their interests. However, people often worry that big contributors to a candidate will receive special favors if he or she wins. To limit political contributions, Congress passed the Federal Election Campaign Act (FECA) in 1972. In 2002, Congress passed the Bipartisan Campaign Reform Act (BCRA), which revised the contribution limits.

The BCRA requires every political candidate in federal elections to report the name of each person who contributes $200 or more in a year. The law limits individual contributions to candidates to $2,100 for primary elections and another $2,100 for general elections. The Federal Election Commission enforces these laws.

From *Civics in Practice*, The Citizen in Government

Details or examples from the text	Generalization
_____	_____
_____	_____
_____	_____
_____	_____
_____	_____
_____	_____
_____	_____
_____	_____
_____	_____
_____	_____

Making Generalizations

Reading Skills

Reading Economics

As you read about economics you will come across a lot of new information. Making generalizations will help you sort through the details and focus on the main points of the text.

YOU TRY IT!

Read the following passage. Then use the graphic organizer below to make a generalization. Be sure to check that your generalization is valid and applies to different situations.

Developing Nations and Natural Resources

Developing nations tend to specialize in the production of one or a few goods, usually, agricultural products or raw materials. Although specialization tends to promote international trade, it can also lead to one-crop economies.

A nation that concentrates on the production of a single item has a one-crop economy. When referring to one-crop economies, economists use the term crop to include many nonagricultural products, such as minerals. One-crop economies often are unstable because the entire economy depends on the world price for a single product.

Environmental factors also may limit growth in a one-crop economy. Suppose that a country specializing in coffee production experiences a severe winter. If a freeze destroys the crop, producers will not be able to supply coffee to the market. Because the country generates few other products that might provide income, its economy will be weakened.

From *Holt Economics*, Developing Countries

Details or examples from the text	Generalization
_____	_____
_____	_____
_____	_____
_____	_____
_____ ▶	_____
_____	_____
_____	_____
_____	_____
_____	_____

Thinking about Content Reading

How to Use Think-Alouds

THINK-ALOUDS

It happens all the time. Your teacher asks the class to tell something about the reading and is met with a classroom full of blank stares. Your classmates' eyes may have followed the words from left to right without paying attention to what the words mean. In other words, they haven't been thinking about what they are reading. This is where a strategy called Think-Aloud can help.

Think-Alouds are one of the best ways to improve reading comprehension. How do they work? In a Think-Aloud, you pause in your reading from time to time to think aloud about what you are reading. It's like having a conversation with the text.

There are many different types of Think-Alouds. Some will help you predict what will happen next, create a picture of the text, make comparisons, or identify problems and solutions. Others will allow you to connect with what you already know, make comments, or question the text. Each type, however, will give you the opportunity to check your understanding as you read.

HOW TO USE THINK-ALOUDS WITH A PARTNER

Large groups, small groups, and individual readers can use the Think-Aloud strategy to react and respond to the text. Use the steps below to complete the Think-Aloud activities in this book with a partner.

1. **Review the Types of Think-Alouds:** Prepare to read and think aloud by reading the Types of Think-Aloud Comments chart on page 80 of this book.

2. **Pair-up:** Find a partner to work with. Decide which one of you will be the designated reader; the other will be the designated listener.

3. **Read and Think-Aloud:** The reader begins to read the excerpt aloud, pausing to make comments for each numbered item. Readers should make sure that they give a verbal or visual cue, such as making eye contact, when switching from reading to thinking aloud.

4. **Take Notes:** As the reader reads and thinks aloud, the listener should jot down the comments the reader makes.

5. **Switch Roles:** Half way through the reading, switch roles with your partner.

6. **Identify and Discuss:** After reading, use the Types of Think-Aloud Comments chart on page 80 to identify which types of comments were made and why.

SAMPLE THINK-ALOUD

Reading World History   Think-Alouds

Model 1

Text   **Comments**

SCIENCE AND RELIGION

The Roman Catholic Church was a powerful force in Europe during the time of the Scientific Revolution. The birth and growth of science led to conflicts between scientists and the Church.[1]

1 *It sounds like I'm going to read about conflicts between scientists and the Church; Type of Think-Aloud: Predicting what happens next.*

There were two related parts to the conflict between science and the Church. The first was that the new science was putting forth ideas that contradicted Church teachings. For example, Copernicus's idea that the earth orbited the sun contradicted the Church teaching that the earth was at the center of the universe.

A second part of the conflict was related to the first. When people contradicted the Church's teachings, they weakened the Church.[2] Church officials were afraid that questioning even one Church teaching might lead to more and more questions about the Church. People might even start to doubt key elements of the faith. Church officials feared this would undermine the Church's influence.[3]

2 *How could they do that? I'd better read to find out; Type of Think-Aloud: Questioning.*

3 *I don't know what "undermine" means. But I guess it means something like "hurt" because Church officials feared it; Type of Think-Aloud: Identifying and fixing problems of understanding.*

The conflict between science and the Church was illustrated by a trial. Galileo published a book that supported the view that the planets orbit the sun. For this, he was put on trial by the Inquisition, a Church court that investigated people who questioned Church authority.

Catholic officials insisted that Galileo publicly reject his findings and accept Catholic teachings that the earth was the center of the universe and did not move. Under threat of torture, Galileo agreed.[4] Still, legend has it that as Galileo left his trial, he muttered, "And yet it does move."

4 *I can see that Galileo must have been scared. I wonder what I would have done if I had been threatened; Type of Think-Aloud: Picturing the text and Making comparisons.*

From *World History,* The Scientific Revolution

85   Thinking about Content Reading

Types of Think-Aloud Comments

Predicting what happens next	"It sounds like I'm going to learn about . . ." "I think this is going to be about . . ." "I bet I'm going to read about . . ."
Picturing the text	"From this part here, I can see that . . ." "I imagine that . . ."
Making comparisons	"This reminds me of . . ." "This sounds like . . ." "This is similar to . . ."
Identifying and fixing problems in understanding	"I don't get this. Maybe I'd better . . ." "I don't know what this means. What if . . ." "This is difficult. I'd better consider . . ."
Connecting	"I know this part is right because . . ." "This reminds me of . . ." "I already know . . ."
Making comments	"I like this part because . . ." "I think this means that . . ." "This part describes well . . ."
Questioning	"I wonder why . . ." "How could . . ." "What does the author mean by . . ."

Thinking about Content Reading

Text

Comments

MAXIMIZING PROFITS AND EFFICIENCY

During the late 1800s, several factors led to a decline in the quality of working conditions.[1] Machines run by unskilled workers were eliminating the jobs of many skilled craftspeople. These low-paid workers could be replaced easily. Factories began to focus on specialization, or workers repeating a single step again and again. Specialization brought costs down and caused production to rise. But it also made workers tired, bored, and more likely to be injured.[2] Specialization allowed for Henry Ford's idea of a moving assembly line to speed production. Ford's use of the moving assembly line allowed automobiles to be made more quickly and cheaply. Automobiles soon became available to a wider segment of the population than ever before.

In 1909 Frederick W. Taylor, an efficiency engineer, published a popular book called *The Principles of Scientific Management*.[3] He encouraged managers to view workers as interchangeable parts of the production process. In factories, managers influenced by Taylor paid less attention to working conditions. Injuries increased, and as conditions grew worse, workers looked for ways to bring about change.

From *United States History*, The Industrial Age

1 _____

2 _____

3 _____

Text

Comments

JEFFERSON OPPOSES THE BANK

Both Jefferson and Madison believed that Hamilton's plans for the economy gave too much power to the federal government.[1] They also thought the U.S. Constitution did not give Congress the power to create a bank. But Hamilton quoted the elastic clause, which states that Congress can "make all laws which shall be necessary and proper" to govern the nation.

Hamilton declared that the clause allowed the government to create a national bank. Hamilton believed in loose construction of the Constitution. Loose construction means that the federal government can take reasonable actions that the Constitution does not specifically forbid.[2]

Jefferson thought that the elastic clause should be used only in special cases. He wrote to President Washington, "The Constitution allows only the means which are 'necessary,' not those which are merely 'convenient.'" Jefferson believed in strict construction of the Constitution. People who favor strict construction think that the federal government should do only what the Constitution specifically says it can do.

President Washington and Congress agreed with Hamilton.[3] They hoped a bank would offer stability for the U.S. economy. In February 1791 Congress enacted the charter for the Bank of the United States—the country's first national bank. The bank played an important role in making the U.S. economy more stable.

From *United States History*, Launching the Nation

1 _____
_____
_____
_____
_____

2 _____
_____
_____
_____
_____

3 _____
_____
_____
_____
_____

Text

RUSH TO CALIFORNIA

The mass migration to California of miners—and businesspeople who made money off the miners—is known as the gold rush.[1] The migrants who left for California in 1849 were called forty-niners. Their numbers approached a stunning 80,000 people.

Many more soon followed. Although the dream of finding gold brought people from around the world, three-fourths of those arriving in California came from the United States. To reach California, most people traveled over land, following the California Trail. Others booked passage on ships that sailed all the way around the southern tip of South America. Still others sailed south to Panama, crossed Central America by mule train, and then sailed north to California. By 1854 a full 300,000 people had migrated to California.

Upon reaching California, most miners moved into camps in the gold fields. Many others—especially businesspeople—settled in cities. San Francisco, the port nearest the gold fields, had a population of about 200 in 1848. One year later some 25,000 people lived there.[2] By 1860 it was home to some 60,000 people.

The town of Stockton, located on the San Joaquin River on the way to the southern gold fields, boomed. Sacramento, located on the Sacramento River between San Francisco and the northern gold fields, also grew rapidly. When California became the thirty-first state in 1850, Sacramento became its capital.[3]

From *American Anthem*, Expansion Leads to Conflict

1 _____
_____
_____
_____
_____

2 _____
_____
_____
_____
_____

3 _____
_____
_____
_____
_____

Text

Comments

CONSERVING FOOD AND OTHER GOODS

Meeting the food needs of the military took top priority in the United States. The planting of victory gardens was one way in which Americans filled these needs.[1]

1 _____

Victory gardens alone did not solve all the nation's food needs. Some foods could not be produced in home gardens, and there was simply not enough of certain products to go around. As a result, the United States began rationing food shortly after the nation entered the war. Rationing means limiting the amount of a certain product each individual can get.

During the war, the government rationed products such as coffee, butter, sugar, and meat. Each member of the family received a ration book, which entitled that person to a certain amount of certain foods. Most people willingly accepted the system. Penalties for breaking the rationing rules could be severe.[2]

2 _____

The war effort also meant shortages of other materials, such as metal, glass, rubber, and gasoline. Gasoline was rationed. Americans helped meet the demand for other materials by holding scrap drives, in which citizens collected waste material of all sorts that might be used in the war efforts. Empty tin cans, bits of rubber and glass—anything that could be useful was salvaged.[3] Even women's silk and nylon stockings were recycled to make parachutes.

3 _____

Scrap drives provided a way for young Americans to help with the war effort. Scouts and other youth organizations helped lead the way in this important national effort.

From *American Anthem*, The United States in World War II

Thinking about Content Reading

Text

SCIENCE AND RELIGION

The Roman Catholic Church was a powerful force in Europe during the time of the Scientific Revolution. The birth and growth of science led to conflicts between scientists and the Church.[1]

There were two related parts to the conflict between science and the Church. The first was that the new science was putting forth ideas that contradicted Church teachings. For example, Copernicus's idea that the earth orbited the sun contradicted the Church teaching that the earth was at the center of the universe.[2]

A second part of the conflict was related to the first. When people contradicted the Church's teachings, they weakened the Church. Church officials were afraid that questioning even one Church teaching might lead to more and more questions about the Church. People might even start to doubt key elements of the faith. Church officials feared this would undermine the Church's influence.

The conflict between science and the Church was illustrated by a trial. Galileo published a book that supported the view that the planets orbit the sun. For this, he was put on trial by the Inquisition, a Church court that investigated people who questioned Church authority.[3]

Catholic officials insisted that Galileo publicly reject his findings and accept Catholic teachings that the earth was the center of the universe and did not move. Under threat of torture, Galileo agreed.[6] Still, legend has it that as Galileo left his trial, he muttered, "And yet it does move."

From *World History*, The Scientific Revolution

1 _____
_____
_____
_____
_____

2 _____
_____
_____
_____

3 _____
_____
_____
_____

Text

Comments

ARISTOCRATS AND TYRANTS RULE

Greece is the birthplace of democracy, a type of government in which people rule themselves. The word democracy comes from Greek words meaning "rule of the people." But Greek city-states didn't start as democracies, and not all became democratic.[1]

Even Athens, the city where democracy was born, began with a different kind of government. In early Athens, kings ruled the city-state. Later, a group of rich landowners, or aristocrats, took power. A government in which only a few people have power is called an oligarchy.

The aristocrats dominated Athenian society. As the richest men in town, they ran the city's economy. They also served as its generals and judges. Common people had little say in the government.[2]

In the 600s BC a group of rebels tried to overthrow the aristocrats. They failed. Possibly as a result of their attempt, however, a man named Draco created a new set of laws for Athens. These laws were very harsh. For example, Draco's laws made minor crimes such as loitering punishable by death.

The people of Athens thought Draco's laws were too strict. In the 590s BC a man named Solon created a set of laws that were much less harsh and gave more rights to nonaristocrats. Under Solon's laws, all free men living in Athens became citizens, people who had the right to participate in government.[3] But his efforts were not enough for Athenians. They were ready to end the rule of the aristocracy.

From *World History*, Ancient Greece

1 _____
_____
_____
_____
_____

2 _____
_____
_____
_____
_____

3 _____
_____
_____
_____
_____

Text

Comments

GHANA BUILDS AN EMPIRE

By 800 Ghana was firmly in control of West Africa's trade routes. Nearly all trade between northern and southern Africa passed through Ghana. Ghana's army kept the trade routes safe. Trade increased, and so did Ghana's wealth.[1]

With so many traders passing through their lands, Ghana's rulers looked for ways to profit from their dealings. One way was to force every trader who entered Ghana to pay a special tax on the goods he carried. Then each trader had to pay another tax on the goods he took with him when he left. The people of Ghana also had to pay taxes. In addition, Ghana forced small neighboring tribes to pay tribute.

Ghana's gold mines brought even more income into the royal treasury. Some gold was carried by traders to lands as far away as England.[2] But not all of Ghana's gold was traded. Ghana's kings also kept huge stores of the precious metal for themselves.

The rulers of Ghana banned everyone else in Ghana from owning gold nuggets. Common people could only own gold dust, which they used as money.[3] This ensured that the king was richer than his subjects.

Part of Ghana's wealth went to support its powerful army. Ghana's kings used this army to conquer many neighboring areas. To keep order in their large empire, Ghana's kings allowed conquered rulers to retain much of their power. These local rulers acted as governors of their territories, answering only to the king.

From *World History*, Early African Civilizations

1 _____
_____
_____
_____
_____

2 _____
_____
_____
_____
_____

3 _____
_____
_____
_____
_____

Text

Comments

THE MONGOL EMPIRE

Among the nomadic people who attacked the Chinese were the Mongols. For centuries, the Mongols had lived as separate tribes in the vast plains north of China. Then in 1206, a powerful leader, or khan, united them. His name was Temüjin. When he became leader, though, he was given a new title: "Universal Ruler," or Genghis Khan.[1]

Genghis Khan organized the Mongols into a powerful army and led them on bloody expeditions of conquest. The brutality of the Mongol attacks terrorized people throughout much of Asia and Eastern Europe. Genghis Khan and his army killed all of the men, women, and children in countless cities and villages.[2] Within 20 years, he ruled a large part of Asia.

Genghis Khan then turned his attention to China. He first led his armies into northern China in 1211. They fought their way south, wrecking whole towns and ruining farmland. By the time of Genghis Khan's death in 1227, all of northern China was under Mongol control.

The Mongol conquests did not end with Genghis Khan's death, though. His sons and grandsons continued to raid lands all over Asia and Eastern Europe . . .

In 1260 Genghis Khan's granson Kublai Khan became ruler of the Mongol Empire. He completed the conquest of China and in 1279 declared himself emperor of China. This began the Yuan dynasty, a period that some people also call the Mongol Ascendancy.[3] For the first time in its long history, foreigners ruled all of China.

From *World History*, China

1 _____
_____
_____
_____
_____

2 _____
_____
_____
_____
_____

3 _____
_____
_____
_____
_____

Text

Comments

CUBA

Cuba is the largest and most populous country in the Caribbean. It is located just 92 miles (148 km) south of Florida. Havana, the capital, is the country's largest and most important city.

Cuba has been run by a Communist government since Fidel Castro came to power in 1959.[1] At that time, the government took over banks, large sugarcane plantations, and other businesses. Many of these businesses were owned by U.S. companies. Because of the takeovers, the U.S. government banned trade with Cuba and restricted travel there by U.S. citizens.

Today the government still controls the economy. Most of Cuba's farms are organized as cooperatives or government-owned plantations. A cooperative is an organization owned by its members and operated for their mutual benefit.[2]

Besides controlling the economy, Cuba's government also controls all the newspapers, television, and radio stations. While many Cubans support Castro and his policies, others oppose them.[3] Some people who oppose Castro have become refugees in the United States. Many Cuban refugees have become U.S. citizens.

From *The Americas*, Central America and the Caribbean

1 _____
_____
_____
_____
_____

2 _____
_____
_____
_____
_____

3 _____
_____
_____
_____

Text

Comments

WIND, WATER, AND STORMS

If you watch weather reports, you will hear about storms moving across the United States.[1] Tracking storms is important to us because the United States has so many of them. As you will see, some areas of the world have more storms than others do.

Most storms occur when two air masses collide. An air mass is a large body of air. The place where two air masses of different temperatures or moisture content meet is a front. Air masses frequently collide in regions like the United States, where the westerlies meet the polar easterlies.[2]

Fronts can produce rain or snow as well as severe weather such as thunderstorms and icy blizzards. Thunderstorms produce rain, lightning, and thunder. In the United states, they are most common in spring and summer. Blizzards produce strong winds and large amounts of snow and are most common during winter.

Thunderstorms and blizzards can also produce tornadoes, another type of severe storm. A tornado is a small, rapidly twisting funnel of air that touches the ground. Tornadoes usually affect a limited area and last only a few minutes. However, they can be highly destructive, uprooting trees and tossing large vehicles through the air.[3] Tornadoes can be extremely deadly as well . . .

The largest and most destructive storms, however, are hurricanes. These large, rotating storms form over tropical waters in the Atlantic Ocean, usually from late sumer to fall. Did you know that hurricanes and typhoons are the same? Typhoons are just hurricanes that form in the Pacific Ocean.

From *Introduction to Geography*, Climate, Environment, and Resources

1 _____
_____
_____
_____
_____

2 _____
_____
_____
_____
_____

3 _____
_____
_____
_____
_____

Thinking about Content Reading

Text

Comments

ECONOMY

The level of economic development in the Indian Perimeter is generally low. The countries depend heavily on agriculture.[1] Most have tried to build new industries. However, these efforts have been slowed by a lack of natural resources. Despite these similarities, there is quite a range between the richest and poorest countries of the region. For example, Nepal and Bhutan are among the poorest countries in the world. Yet Pakistan, while still a poor country, has experienced growth in GDP since independence.[2]

Pakistan has used its significant mineral resources to help develop its manufacturing industries. However, nearly half the labor force still works in agriculture. Although Pakistan's economy has grown, so has its population. This population growth strains the country's ability to provide basic services to its people.

Bangladesh is overwhelmingly agricultural. More than half of the people work in farming. Jute, rice, and tea are the most important crops. Farming depends on the monsoon. Variations in the timing and intensity of the monsoon rains make the difference between a good harvest or a poor one.[3] In recent times people have built a number of irrigation projects to control floods and conserve water for the dry months. These projects, the increased use of fertilizers, and new crops have increased farm output.

From *World Geography Today*, The Indian Perimeter

1 _____
_____
_____
_____
_____

2 _____
_____
_____
_____
_____

3 _____
_____
_____
_____

Text

Comments

NATURAL INCREASE

Geographers are interested in the rate of natural population growth, or natural increase. This rate is based just on births and deaths—it does not take migration into account.[1] You can find the rate by subtracting the death rate from the birthrate. This final number is expressed as a percentage. In the United States, the rate of natural increase is about 0.6 percent each year.

The rate of natural increase varies greatly in countries around the world. The highest rates are found in countries in Africa and Southwest Asia. Rates there are sometimes 3 percent or higher.[2] The number of people living in those places is rising rapidly. Most countries in Central and South America and in Southeast Asia have more moderate rates of natural increase. The rates for these areas are somewhere between 1 and 3 percent. The lowest rates—less than 1 percent—are found in most European and North American countries. Australia, New Zealand, and Japan also have such low rates. Some countries, such as Italy and Russia, actually have negative growth rates.[3] The number of people living in these countries is decreasing.

These percentages—1, 2, and 3—may sound small. However, they can add up to large population increases in a short period of time. For example, suppose the number of people living in a country grows at a rate of 3 percent. That country's population will double in only about 23 years! Geographers call the number of years needed to double a country's population its doubling time.

1 _____
_____
_____
_____
_____

2 _____
_____
_____
_____
_____

3 _____
_____
_____
_____
_____
_____

From *World Geography Today*, Human Geography

Text   **Comments**

CONGRESS AND THE CONSTITUTION

Congress often applies the Constitution to a particular issue in society.[1] It does this by interpreting whether some passage, or clause, in the Constitution gives Congress the authority to pass a particular law.

1 _____
_____
_____
_____
_____

For example, the Constitution says nothing about whether all workers should earn a minimum wage. However, the Constitution does give Congress the power to control trade among the states. Goods made by workers usually travel from one state to another. So Congress decided that the Constitution gives it the power to pass laws affecting working conditions nationwide, including wage rates.[2] It then wrote laws establishing a minimum wage.

2 _____
_____
_____
_____
_____

The Supreme Court has the power to decide if Congress has interpreted the Constitution correctly. The Court's interpretation is final. If the Supreme Court rules that a law is unconstitutional, the law is dead. If the Court upholds the law, it remains in effect.

If the Supreme Court declares an act of Congress unconstitutional, Congress may rewrite the law. If Congress overcomes the Court's objections, the new law will stand.

For example, Congress may not pass bills of attainder (laws which punish a person without a jury trial) or ex post facto laws (which make an act a crime after the act has been committed).[3] Congress also may not suspend the writ of habeas corpus (a court order requiring the government to bring a prisoner to court and explain why he or she is being held).

3 _____
_____
_____
_____
_____

From *Civics in Practice*, The United States Constitution

Text

Comments

THE HOUSE OF REPRESENTATIVES

According to the Constitution, the number of representatives each state can elect to the House is based on the state's population.[1] Each state is entitled to at least one representative. Washington, D.C., Guam, American Samoa, and the Virgin Islands each have one nonvoting delegate in the House.

Today there are 435 members in the House. Why 435 members? In 1789, when the first Congress met, the Constitution allowed for 65 representatives in the House. Each state elected one representative for every 30,000 people in the state. However, as new states joined the Union and the population increased, membership in the House kept growing. Eventually, Congress had to limit the size of the House to 435 members.[2]

Every 10 years, after the census is taken, Congress determines how the seats in the House are to be apportioned, or distributed. If a state's population decreases, the number of its representatives may be reduced. States whose populations grow may be entitled to more representatives.

Voters elect their representative according to the congressional district in which they live.[3] Each state's legislature is responsible for dividing the state into as many congressional districts as it has members in the House of Representatives. District boundaries must be drawn so that each district is almost equal in population.

From *Civics in Practice*, The Legislative Branch

1 _____
_____
_____
_____
_____

2 _____
_____
_____
_____
_____

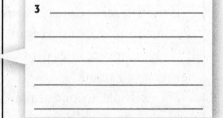

3 _____
_____
_____
_____
_____

Text

Comments

THE VICE PRESIDENCY

For much of the country's history, a vice president had very little to do. What are the responsibilities of the modern vice president?[1] One very important responsibility is to serve as president if the president dies, leaves office, or is unable to fulfill his or her duties. Eight presidents have died while in office and one president resigned. In each case, the vice president was sworn in as president. The vice president also serves a four-year term and must meet the same constitutional qualifications as the president. The vice president receives a salary of $186,300 a year, plus a $10,000 taxable expense allowance.[2]

The vice president has only one other job defined in the Constitution—to preside over the Senate. However, the vice president is not a member of the Senate. He or she cannot take part in Senate debates and may vote only in the case of a tie.

In recent years, presidents have given their vice presidents more responsibilities than those described by the Constitution. Presidents often send their vice presidents to represent the United States overseas. Vice presidents usually work closely with the president in order to be fully informed on the issues. For example, Vice President Dick Cheney has an important role on President Bush's team, becoming involved in developing policy and in gathering support for the president's programs.[3]

From *Civics in Practice*, The Executive Branch

1 _____

2 _____

3 _____

Thinking about Content Reading

Text

Comments

A NATION OF LAWS

There are two basic categories of laws, criminal law and civil law.[1] When people talk about "breaking the law," they are usually referring to a crime. A crime is any behavior that is illegal because society, through its government, considers the behavior harmful to society. Criminal law refers to the group of laws that define what acts are crimes. Criminal law also describes how a person accused of a crime should be tried in court and how crimes should be punished.

Criminal laws are intended to protect society as a whole. For example, laws against assault, murder, and rape help protect you and other people from being harmed. Laws against stealing help protect your property and other people's property as well. You might think that a crime against another person does not affect you, but that is not true.[2] If someone who breaks into your neighbor's house and steals something is not caught and punished, the criminal may steal again. The criminal might even break into your house next. And if criminals are not caught and punished, people may begin to think that it is okay to steal.

The other basic category of laws is civil law. Civil law is the group of laws that refer to disputes between people. If you have a dispute with someone and you cannot solve it privately, you may go to court to settle the matter. In court, the judge and maybe a jury will listen to the facts of the case. The judge will then apply the civil law and make a decision. Civil laws are used to settle a wide range of personal issues, such as contract disputes, divorce proceedings, and property boundaries.[3]

From *Civics in Practice*, The Judicial Branch

1 _____
_____
_____
_____
_____

2 _____
_____
_____
_____
_____

3 _____
_____
_____
_____
_____

Text

Comments

TYPES OF ECONOMIC SYSTEMS

You know that scarcity affects all aspects of economics and that it requires economic actors—individuals, businesses, and governments—to make choices.[1] You, for example, have a limited amount of money and time—a basic economic problem. This scarcity forces you to make choices among ways to spend your money and your time—another common economic problem. In other worlds, scarcity results from the combination of limited resources and unlimited wants.

Nations also must make choices in order to use their natural, human, capital and entrepreneurial resources efficiently. A nation—or, more directly, its leaders—must address the three basic economic questions: what to produce, how to produce, and for whom to produce.[2]

A nation's responses to these questions are determined by its economic system. And economic system reflects the process of a nation—or any society—follows to produce goods and services. There are four types of economic systems: traditional command, market, and mixed.

In truth, all economies are mixed. Pure traditional, pure command and pure market systems are models that do not exist in the world today. [3]

From *Holt Economics*, Economic Systems

1 _____
_____
_____
_____

2 _____
_____
_____
_____
_____

3 _____
_____
_____
_____

Text

Comments

COMPETITION

Competition tends to increase supply, while a lack of competition tends to decrease supply. Why is this so?[1]

Consider the market for home video games. When the first company offered these games, the selection was extremely limited. Demand for these games rose quickly, however, generating high sales and good profits for the company. These profits encouraged dozens of new video firms to enter the market. The supply and selection of games soon skyrocketed.[2]

As this example shows, a larger number of suppliers in a market tends to increase supply. Each producer competes for a share of the market demand by supplying more of the product. This shifts the supply curve to the right as producers offer more goods at each and every price for the product. Remember that suppliers can leave as well as enter a market. If the demand for video games were to fall, there would be more games (more supply) on the market than consumers wanted to purchase.[3] Supply would be higher than demand. Some companies would not sell all of their games and might not make enough profit. These companies might then leave the market. Supply would shrink as fewer producers competed to deliver games to the market.

From *Holt Economics*, Supply

1 _____
_____
_____
_____
_____

2 _____
_____
_____
_____
_____

3 _____
_____
_____
_____
_____

Thinking about Content Reading

Text

Comments

ECONOMIC DEVELOPMENT

In the world today there are nearly 200 nations, all at different stages of economic development.[1] Economic development is a broad term that includes the size and sophistication of a nation's industrial, service, technical, and agricultural sectors.

The industrialized nations of the world, which economists generally classify as developed nations, have a high level of industrial and technical expertise, as well as a variety of economic institutions, such as banking systems, stock markets, and trade networks. The World Bank—an international economic organization—has classified some 39 nations as being "high income" or highly developed.[2] The United States, Canada, Japan, most nations in Europe, and several other nations in Asia and the Middle East are among the developed nations. The combined populations of the developed nations make up less than one sixth of the world's population.

Economists classify the remaining nations of the world as developing nations. The majority of the world's population lives in these developing nations.[3] Developing nations are characterized by low per capita gross nation income (GNI, also called the gross national product or GNP), limited resources or inefficient use of resources, rapid population growth rate, and a dependency on agriculture as the main form of production.

From *Holt Economics*, Developing Countries

1 _____
_____
_____
_____
_____

2 _____
_____
_____
_____
_____

3 _____
_____
_____
_____
_____

Thinking about Content Reading

Text

Comments

THE EUROPEAN UNION

In the early 1990s many Europeans feared that the elimination of trade barriers among European nations would lead to a single European economy and society.[1] Instead of creating a group of distinct nations each with its own language and customs, these people argued, free trade would blur populations—and eventually cultures.

So far, these fears have not materialized. Economists have instead noted increasing specialization based on traditional centers of production.[2] For example, before the European Union (EU) was established, Carrara, Italy, was a marble—carving center for centuries, even long after its quarries were depleted. After the EU was formed, Carrara's carving industry was not challenged by new marble-carving centers. In fact, Carrara remains among the leading marble-carving centers in Europe despite the fact that lowered trade barriers also allow marble to be imported to Naples, Marseilles, or any other location in Europe.[3]

Similarly moviemakers in Spain have tried to establish a film animation industry in the city of Seville. Film animators continue to flock to London's Soho district, however, where artists and filmmakers have centered their activity for years.

From *Holt Economics*, International Trade

1 _____
_____
_____
_____
_____

2 _____
_____
_____
_____
_____

3 _____
_____
_____
_____
_____

How to Use Graphic Organizers

Graphic organizers are a valuable tool for reading and studying social studies because they provide many different ways to organize information. Each graphic organizer in this chart can be used with any social studies subject.

Type of Graphic Organizer	Suggested Uses
Web Diagram	• Identifying details about historical figures or events, etc. • Identifying qualities of natural formations, etc. • Identifying cultural or physical features of a country, etc.
Cause and Effect Diagram	• Explaining the cause and effect of a historical event, such as World War 1 • Analyzing the cause of a geographic occurrence, such as land erosion • Explaining the cause and effect of an economic situation, such as a recession

Type of Graphic Organizer	Suggested Uses
Cause and Effect Chain 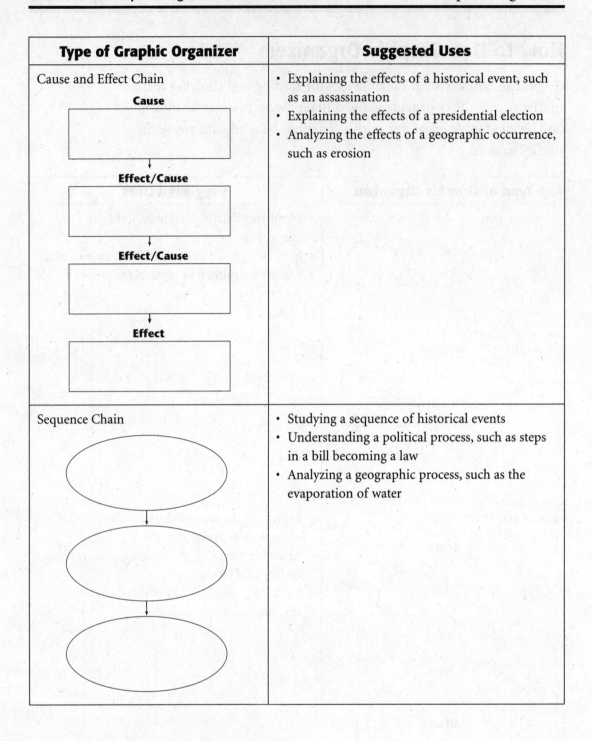	• Explaining the effects of a historical event, such as an assassination • Explaining the effects of a presidential election • Analyzing the effects of a geographic occurrence, such as erosion
Sequence Chain	• Studying a sequence of historical events • Understanding a political process, such as steps in a bill becoming a law • Analyzing a geographic process, such as the evaporation of water

Type of Graphic Organizer	Suggested Uses
Comparison-Contrast Chart 		(Subject 1)	(Subject 2)
---	---	---
(Point A)		
(Point B)		
(Point C)		
(Point D)				• Comparing/contrasting causes and effects of two battles or wars • Comparing/contrasting two economic or political systems • Comparing/contrasting resources in different locations
Venn Diagram	• Comparing/contrasting historical figures, time periods, etc. • Comparing/contrasting countries, regions, cities, etc. • Analyzing two trends, systems, laws, etc.
Main Idea and Details Chart **Main Idea** **Supporting Detail 1** **Supporting Detail 2** **Supporting Detail 3**	• Identifying main ideas and details about historical figures, time periods, etc. • Forming main ideas and details about countries, regions, cities, etc. • Understanding main ideas and details about economic conditions, governmental structures, etc.

Type of Graphic Organizer	Suggested Uses
Determining Main Idea Chart Topic Important Details Main Idea Topic Important Details Main Idea	• Studying details about a topic, such as inflation or capitalism, to arrive at a main idea • Using details about a historical event or a culture to arrive at a main idea • Examining details about a topic, such as migration or population, to arrive at a main idea
KWL Chart Topic: _____ | K What I *Know*	W What I *Want* to Learn	L What I Have *Learned*
---|---|---|	• Reading about historical figures, time periods, etc. • Studying countries, regions, cities, etc. • Researching political issues, legal topics, etc.
Positive-Negative Chart Positive Negative	• Evaluating positive and negative effects of a change in power • Judging good and bad consequences of changing the environment • Evaluating pros and cons of changing requirements for citizenship

Type of Graphic Organizer	Suggested Uses
Evaluation Pyramid	• Evaluating the importance of reasons for the rise and fall of an empire • Ranking most important U.S. presidents • Judging the most important factors in a country's economy
Conclusions Chart	• Drawing conclusions about the effects of agricultural practices • Determining the effectiveness of a leader • Drawing conclusions about the effect of a law